MACMILLAN ACADEMIC SKILLS

Skillful
Reading&Writing

Teacher's Book

1

Author: Stacey H. Hughes
Series Consultant: Dorothy E. Zemach

Macmillan Education
4 Crinan Street
London N1 9XW
A division of Macmillan Publishers Limited
Companies and representatives throughout the world

ISBN 978-0-230-42979-6

Designed by eMC Design Limited

Cover design by eMC Design Limited

Page layout by MPS Limited

The Academic Keyword List (AKL) was designed by Magali Paquot
at the Centre for English Corpus Linguistics, Université catholique
de Louvain (Belgium) within the framework of a research project led by
Professor Sylviane Granger http://www.uclouvain.be/en-372126.html.

Authors' acknowledgements
I would like to thank the team at Macmillan for their encouragement
and support.

Please see Student's Book imprint page for visual walkthrough photo
credits. All author photos were kindly supplied by the authors.

The author(s) and publishers are grateful for permission to reprint the
following copyright material:

Material from The Study Skills Handbook by Stella Cottrell, copyright
© Stella Cottrell, 1999, 2003 & 2008, firstpublished by Palgrave
Macmillan, reproduced with permission of the publisher.

Printed and bound in Thailand

2017 2016 2015 2014
10 9 8 7 6 5 4 3 2

Contents

		Reading texts	Reading skills	
UNIT 1	Character Page 7	1 Are you a natural leader? **Psychology** 2 The hero within **Literary studies**	**Pre-reading** Previewing	**Close** Using pronouns
UNIT 2	Time Page 17	1 A matter of time **Human behavior** 2 What time is it? **History**	**Close** Identifying the author's purpose	**Global** Skimming
UNIT 3	Home Page 27	1 Home is where the heart is **Anthropology** 2 Home automation **Technology**	**Close** Highlighting	**Close** Annotating
UNIT 4	Size Page 37	1 Fuel of the sea **Ecology** 2 Size doesn't matter **Urban planning**	**Pre-reading** Predicting	**Close** Making inferences
UNIT 5	Patterns Page 47	1 Time for a change **Psychology** 2 The Fibonacci sequence **Mathematics**	**Close** Determining main ideas and supporting details	**Close** Taking notes
UNIT 6	Speed Page 57	1 Hurry up and slow down! **Sociology** 2 Keeping up with the Tarahumara **Anthropology**	**Close** Distinguishing facts from opinions	**Close** Identifying tone
UNIT 7	Vision Page 67	1 Is seeing really believing? **Biology** 2 Color and flags **Semiotics**	**Global** Scanning	**Close** Using a chart to organize your notes
UNIT 8	Extremes Page 77	1 Earth's final frontier **Engineering** 2 Super Sherpa **Environmental studies**	**Close** Finding similarities and differences	**Global** Identifying the source
UNIT 9	Life Page 87	1 Coming of age **Anthropology** 2 Gardening 380 kilometers above Earth **Botany**	**Close** Summarizing	**Close** Identifying reasons
UNIT 10	Work Page 97	1 The farmer's lazy son **Literary studies** 2 Leave it for the robot **Technology**	**Close** Sequencing	**Close** Reading charts and graphs

Vocabulary skill	Grammar	Writing skill	Writing task	Digibook video activity	Study skills
Using examples to find meaning	The simple present tense	Writing topic sentences	Describing a hero	What makes a hero?	Setting up a study space
Organizing new words: nouns and verbs	Verbs followed by infinitives and gerunds	Understanding sentence patterns	Describing how to achieve a goal	Time flies as you get older	Writing for the fearful
Using explanations to find meaning	*There is / are* (+ quantifier) + noun	Brainstorming word maps	Describing your home	How our homes have changed	Reviewing and practicing vocabulary
Using definitions to find meaning	The present progressive tense	Writing compound sentences	Describing how your neighborhood is changing	Reaching for the skies	Process writing
Adding prefixes for negation	Giving advice and making suggestions	Using end punctuation and capitalization	Giving advice in an email	Spots and stripes	Where does the time go?
Organizing new words: adjectives and adverbs	Comparative forms of adjectives and adverbs	Using commas and colons	Making a comparison	A need for speed	Keeping a journal
Adding suffixes to change verbs into nouns	Count and noncount nouns	Writing complete sentences	Describing colors	Learning to see	Studying with others
Understanding compound words	Expressing ability	Using transitions to add and emphasize information	Giving your opinion	Pushing the limits	Using computers for effective study
Finding the correct definition of a word	The simple past tense	Using transitions to sequence events	Describing a memorable day	Saving the bees	Making the most of your dictionary
Using collocations	Future forms	Using parallel structure	Describing your future	Work and motivation	Making the most of the library

VOCABULARY PREVIEW Pre-teaching essential vocabulary which appears in both texts within the unit.

BEFORE YOU READ These introductions to the reading topics prepare students for the upcoming subject matter.

GLOBAL READING Global reading is the first time the students will read the text; encouraging them to engage with the big issues and the overall picture.

SKILLS BOXES These focus on the newly-presented skill, why it's important and how to do it. They also highlight reading tips.

CLOSE READING Following on from Global reading is Close reading. This is an in-depth detailed analysis of the text.

Reading Skills

Vocabulary preview

Complete these sentences. Circle the correct meanings of the words in bold.

1 The **background** of a picture is _____ the main part.
   a in front of   b behind
2 If you draw a **horizontal** line, you draw it _____ of the page.
   a across the bottom   b down the side
3 When you **perceive** something, you _____ it.
   a notice   b say
4 If you **restrict** something, you _____ it.
   a limit   b expand
5 To **signal** someone, you might _____.
   a move or make a sound   b think about the person
6 If something **symbolizes** something, it _____ it by a sign.
   a defeats   b represents
7 Something **universal** affects _____ in the world.
   a no one   b everyone
8 If you draw a **vertical** line, you draw it _____ of the page.
   a across the bottom   b down the side

READING 1 Is seeing really believing?

Before you read

Try these experiments. Which takes longer? Why? Discuss with a partner.
1 Read the color words as quickly as you can. Time yourself.
2 Say the colors as quickly as you can. Time yourself.

BLUE	YELLOW	ORANGE
GREEN	BLUE	BLUE
PURPLE	GREEN	ORANGE
ORANGE	YELLOW	GREEN
RED	YELLOW	BLUE
PURPLE	PURPLE	RED
RED	RED	PURPLE
BLUE	YELLOW	ORANGE

Global reading

1 Skim *Is seeing really believing?* Check (✓) what it is mainly about.
   1 ☐ Color and personality   3 ☐ Number puzzles
   2 ☐ Optical illusions   4 ☐ Web design

> **SCANNING**
> Scanning is searching a text to find specific information or key words, such as names, dates, or statistics. Like skimming (unit 2), you do not read every word. You also do not need to start at the beginning of a text. Instead, you can predict where you think the information is and start there.

2 Scan *Is seeing really believing?* Circle the color words.

Close reading

Read *Is seeing really believing?* Correct these false sentences.
1 Color is created by our eyes.
2 Illusion plays a role in how our brain perceives images.
3 In the first illusion, the colors are different.
4 Vision is created according to our past experiences.
5 We all see the world in the same way.

68 UNIT 7 VISION

READING EXCERPTS Interesting and original topics make up the reading excerpts in *Skillful*.

DEVELOPING CRITICAL THINKING Developing critical thinking is a chance to reflect on issues presented in the text.

SENTENCE FRAMES Add support and help for students who lack confidence with their speaking skills.

IS SEEING REALLY BELIEVING?

🏠 HOME   ⚙ BLOG   ✎ CONTACT

Reading Skills

[1] Tomatoes are red, the sky is blue, and bananas are yellow, right? Well, not exactly. Color does not really exist, at least not in a literal or universal sense. What exists is light. Light is real, but color is not. Color is simply created by and restricted to the brain. We know this because colors can look different in our minds.

[2] We're told to trust our eyes, but our eyes just don't have that much to do with vision. We see much more with our brains, and it's easy to play tricks on the brain. We perceive these differences because the brain doesn't necessarily want to see the actual image. Rather, it wants to make sense of the image. The brain does this by looking at the surrounding context.

[3] Look at the two tiles in picture 1. They are identical in color. Now look at what happens when we change their context in picture 2. In their new context, the horizontal and vertical lines look the same, but their colors look different. The context suggests that the dark brown tile on the top shows a poorly reflected surface under bright light. The bright orange tile on the side suggests a highly reflective surface in shadow. You see different colors now because your brain thinks they have a different meaning. This is an example of an optical illusion.

[4] Color is created according to our past experiences. When you see something as an optical illusion, it is because your brain behaves as if the objects in the current images are real, in the same way as images you have seen previously.

[5] Look at the scenes of the desert in picture 3. They have the same color composition of blues and yellows. Now stare at the dot in picture 4 for one minute. Look back at the desert scenes. The reason the colors now appear different is because your brain incorporates the recent history of red on the left and green on the right into the second image, at least for a short time.

[6] This raises the question: Do you see what I see? The answer, in short, is no. Our experiences and histories in the world are different. In fact, none of us even sees the world as it really is, but rather as a meaning derived from our own unique experiences. Seeing is not, in fact, believing.

Developing critical thinking

Discuss these questions in a group.
1 Did the optical illusions work for you? Which was the most interesting?
   Both / Neither of the optical illusions worked for me because ...
2 Describe a situation where you "couldn't believe your eyes"?
   I couldn't believe my eyes when I saw ...
3 Do you think optical illusions are clever or silly? Why?
   In my opinion, optical illusions are clever / silly because ...

ACADEMIC KEYWORDS
derive   (v)   /dɪˈraɪv/
exist   (v)   /ɪɡˈzɪst/
identical (adj) /aɪˈdentɪk(ə)l/

VISION UNIT 7 69

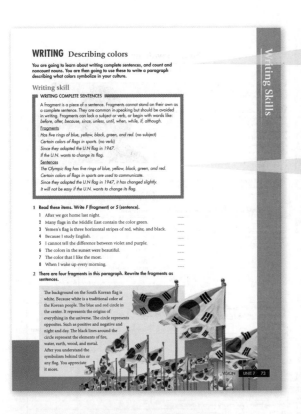

SECTION OVERVIEW Giving students the context within which they are going to study the productive skills.

SKILLS BOXES Highlighting writing advice.

FORM AND FUNCTION Notes on form and function match up with Listening & Speaking grammar in the parallel unit.

END OF UNIT TASK Comprehensive end-of-unit task with a noticing exercise for students to identify key features.

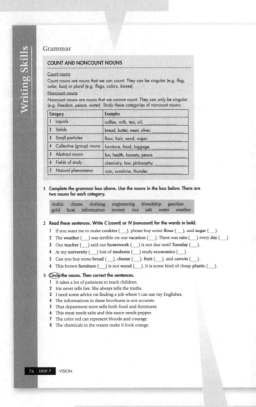

GUIDED PRACTICE Guides students through the stages of a writing task.

WRITING STAGES Gives students support through the stages of the writing process.

STUDY SKILLS WITH STELLA COTTRELL

Information on study skills features at the end of every unit. Some of these pages showcase a task from Stella Cottrell's bestselling title *The Study Skills Handbook*.

Studying with others

by Stella Cottrell

Most courses schedule groupwork of one kind or another because they value the additional learning which takes place.

Contexts

Some of the contexts in which you may be required to work with others include:

- seminars
- discussion groups
- group projects
- support groups
- mentor schemes
- lab groups
- work placements

The format of these will vary, but there are basic principles and skills common to many different group contexts.

Identify one occasion when you were in a group that worked particularly well.

What made the group successful? How did that group differ from other groups you have taken part in?

Working co-operatively

Working co-operatively creates opportunities to:

- share ideas – so each of you has more ideas
- see extra perspectives and points of view, which otherwise you might not have considered
- benefit from a wider pool of experience, background knowledge, and other styles of work
- stimulate each other's thinking
- clarify your own thinking through talking and through answering questions
- gain others' help in staying focused on the main point – so you can explore a thought with the group
- learn to deal with challenge and criticism
- realize there are more dimensions and answers to a question than you can discover on your own

Self-evaluation: studying with other people

Rate yourself on the following aspects of studying with others.

Aspect	1 very weak	2 weak	3 ok	4 good	5 excellent
Appreciating what other people have to offer					
Listening to what other people say					
Making a point effectively in groups					
Understanding how to plan for successful groupwork					
Knowing how to be an effective group member					
Knowing how to deal with difficulties in a group					
Understanding how to deal with unfairness in groups					
Contributing effectively to seminars					
Knowing how to share study without cheating					
Making an effective oral presentation					

STUDY TIPS
Stella offers students useful and memorable tips to improve their studying methods through self-reflection and critiquing.

STUDY SKILLS Making the most of your dictionary

Getting started

Discuss these questions with a partner.

1 How many dictionaries do you own?
2 What kinds of dictionaries have you used?
3 What is the main thing you use a dictionary for? How often do you use one?

Scenario

Read this scenario. Think about what Kwame is doing right and what he is doing wrong.

Consider it

Read these six tips for how to make the most of a dictionary. Discuss each one with a partner. Which ones do you do?

1 **Choose carefully** Not all dictionaries are the same. Decide which type would best serve your needs. For example, do you want a bilingual or English-only dictionary? There are specialist dictionaries to consider as well, such as learner's dictionaries, academic vocabulary dictionaries, and idioms dictionaries.

2 **Get familiar with your dictionary** The best way to familiarize yourself with a dictionary is to read the introduction. This explains how entries are arranged. It also contains useful information on the key abbreviations and pronunciation symbols used in the dictionary.

3 **Be efficient** Try to look up works quickly. Be familiar with alphabetical order and use the guidewords at the top of the page to save time. If you cannot find a word, do not give up. You may need to check other possible spellings of the word.

4 **Locate the correct definition** When you look up a new word, think about how the entries relate to the word. Look for the correct part of speech for the word and decide which definition is correct. The most common meaning is usually placed first.

5 **Study the entry in detail** Besides one or more definitions, a word's entry may include the pronunciation, example sentences, synonyms and antonyms, and other words derived from the same word.

6 **Use the dictionary for other things** You may also find photos and illustrations, maps, lists of famous people, lists of countries and their capitals, flags of countries, and weights and measurements tables.

Over to you

Discuss these questions with a partner.

1 Which of the tips do you follow?
2 How else can you find the meaning of new words?
3 What is one advantage and one disadvantage of electronic dictionaries?

Dictionary /'dɪkʃə,neri/

NOUN [C]

a book that gives an alphabetical list of words with their meanings or their translations

Kwame has been studying English for two years. He uses a bilingual dictionary when he does his homework. He only uses a dictionary to look up words he does not understand. When he looks up a word, he uses the guidewords at the top of the pages to help him find the word quickly. He reads every definition until he finds the correct one. He does not usually check the pronunciation because he is not familiar with the symbols his dictionary uses. He likes to check the example sentences to make sure the definition he chose is the right one. Kwame keeps his dictionary in his study space, but he also keeps a smaller pocket dictionary in his book bag.

STUDY SKILLS SCENARIOS
Using original material, the other end-of-unit study skills task gives students a positive or negative scenario to work through. This provides them with the opportunity for personal performance reflection.

SKILLFUL VERSATILITY Both student and teacher facing, the *Skillful* Digibook can be used for group activities in the classroom, on an Interactive Whiteboard, or by the student alone for homework and extra practice.

DIGIBOOK TOOLBAR The toolbar that appears on each page allows for easy manipulation of the text. Features such as highlighting and a text tool for commenting allow the teacher to add points as the class goes along, and functions like the zoom and grab tool means the teacher can focus students' attention on the appropriate sections.

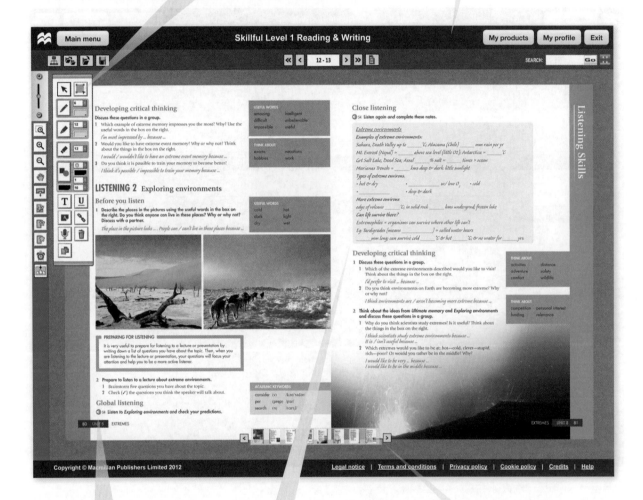

EMBEDDED AUDIO For instant access to the audio for unit exercises, the Digibook has embedded files that you can reach in one click.

PAGE-FAITHFUL Provides a digital replica of *Skillful* Student's Books while hosting additional, interactive features.

EASY NAVIGATION Jumping from section to section isn't a problem with easy page navigation at both the top and bottom of each page.

WHAT IS *SKILLFUL* PRACTICE? The *Skillful* practice area is a student-facing environment designed to encourage extra preparation, and provides additional activities for listening, vocabulary, grammar, speaking, and pronunciation as well as support videos for listening and alternative unit assignments.

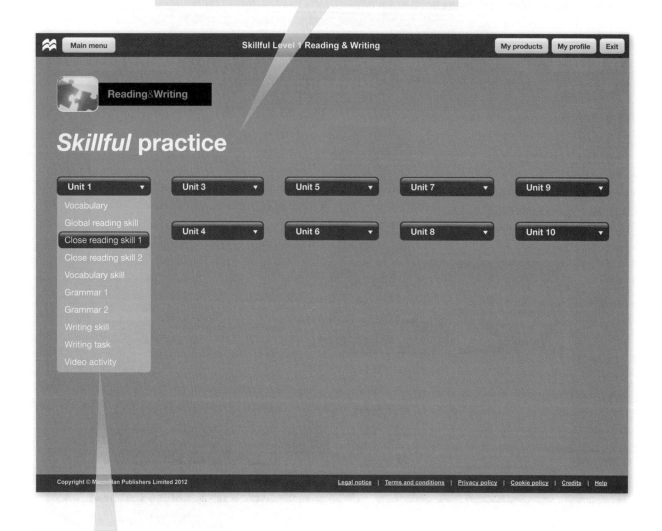

UNIT AND TASK SELECTION
Handy drop-down menus allow students to jump straight to their practice unit and the exercise they want to concentrate on.

TEACHER RESOURCES The *Skillful* teachers have many more resources at their fingertips.

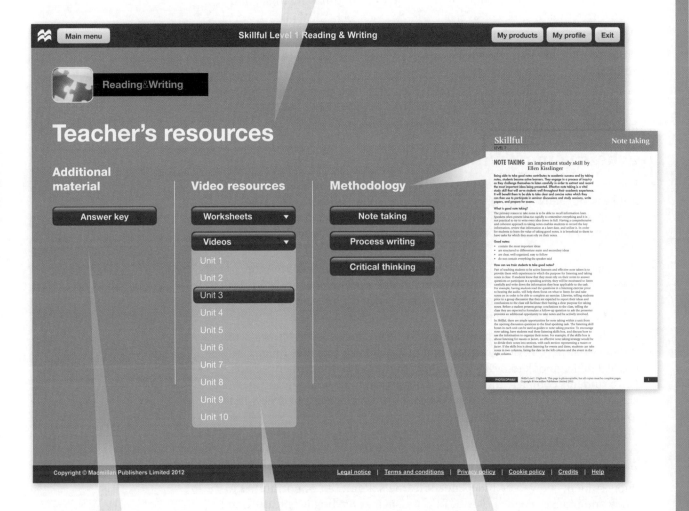

ADDITIONAL MATERIAL Along with the student add-ons there are a plethora of printable worksheets, test materials, and a mark-book functionality to grade and monitor student progress.

VIDEO RESOURCES Teachers have access to the same videos as the students and to complement these there are printable video worksheets to aid lesson planning.

METHODOLOGY For teachers who may need a little extra help to effectively utilize all of the resources *Skillful* has to offer, there are course methodology notes.

To the teacher

Academic success requires so much more than memorizing facts. It takes skills. This means that a successful student can both learn and think critically. *Skillful* helps teachers prepare their students for academic work in English by teaching not only language—vocabulary and grammar—but the necessary skills to engage with topics, texts, and discourse with classmates.

Skillful gives students:

- engaging texts on a wide variety of topics, each examined from two different academic disciplines
- skills for learning about a wide variety of topics from different angles and from different academic areas
- skills they need to succeed when reading and listening to these texts
- skills they need to succeed when writing for and speaking to different audiences
- skills for critically examining the issues presented by a speaker or a writer
- study skills for learning and remembering the English language and important information.

Teachers using *Skillful* should:

- Encourage students to ask questions and interact. Learning a language is not passive. Many of the tasks and exercises involve pairwork, groupwork, and whole-class discussion. Working with others helps students solidify their understanding and challenge and expand their ability to think critically.

- Personalize the material. Help students make connections between the texts in their book and their own world—home, community, and country. Bring in outside material from local sources when it's relevant, making sure it fits the unit topics and language.

- Provide a lot of practice. Have students do each exercise several times, with different partners. Review exercises and material from previous units. Use the *Skillful* Digibook to develop the skills presented in the Student's Book. Have students complete the additional activities on a computer outside of class to make even more progress. Assign frequent manageable review tasks for homework.

- Provide many opportunities for review. Remind students of the skills, grammar, and vocabulary they learned in previous units. Have students study a little bit each day, not just before tests.

- Show students how to be independent learners. Point out opportunities to study and practice English outside of class, such as reading for pleasure and using the Internet in English. Have them find and share information about the different unit topics with the class. The study skills page in every unit gives students valuable tips for successfully managing their own learning.

Learning skills, like learning a language, takes time and practice. Students must be patient with themselves as they put in the necessary time and effort. They should set and check goals. Periodic assessments the teacher can print, such as the unit tests, progress tests, and end test on the Digibook let students see their own progress and measure how much they've learned, so they can feel proud of their academic and linguistic development.

The *Skillful* blend by Dorothy Zemach

In some academic disciplines, students can begin by acquiring a lot of facts and general knowledge. In a language, however, students need far more than information—they need skills. They need to know how to do things: how to explain, persuade, ask for help, extend an invitation, outline and argue a thesis, distinguish between important and unimportant information, follow digressions, understand implied information, and more.

Skillful recognizes that skills such as these can't be learned by memorizing facts. To acquire these skills, students must notice them as they read or listen; break them down and understand them through clear explanations; and then rehearse and apply those skills in carefully scaffolded activities that lead to freer practice.

The listening and reading texts in each unit introduce students to one subject area explored through two different academic disciplines and two distinct genres. Students learn and practice both global skills, such as recognizing tone and identifying the main idea, and close skills, such as understanding pronoun references and figuring out vocabulary from context, to understand the texts on several levels.

These days, students must interact with both digital and printed text, online and offline, in the classroom and in the workplace. The *Skillful* textbooks are therefore supplemented with the *Skillful* Digibooks. These further develop, explain, and extend the skills work found in the printed textbooks. They provide additional exercises related to the skills, the grammar points, and the vocabulary areas. They can be accessed either via the Digibook or through the *Skillful* practice area. Scores are tracked and recorded and if students work offline, their markbook will be updated the next time they connect to the Internet.

Videos for each unit provide additional subject area content that review the skills and language taught in the unit. The videos can be shown in class to feed in additional content and the accompanying worksheets can be used to structure the lesson.

Unit checklists help students keep track of language in the unit and review for tests.

The Digibooks also help teachers with classroom organization and management by assigning and tracking homework and monitoring student progress using the markbook. A full suite of test materials can be used for placement into the appropriate level and then provide end-of-unit tests and end-of-course tests that can be used as both formative assessments (to evaluate progress) and summative assessments (to mark achievements and assign grades). Tests are provided in both editable and non-editable formats enabling teachers to manipulate the content, as desired. The format of these tests is similar to internationally recognized standardized tests.

Dorothy E. Zemach taught ESL for over 18 years, in Asia, Africa, and the US. She holds an MA in TESL and now concentrates on writing and editing ELT materials and conducting teacher training workshops. Her areas of specialty and interest are teaching writing, teaching reading, business English, academic English, and testing.

Teaching study skills by Stella Cottrell

There is a growing awareness that students' performance, even in higher education, can be improved through training in relevant academic skills. Hurley (1994) described study skills as "key skills for all areas of education, including advanced study" and argued that students benefit when these skills are taught explicitly. In other words, it should not be assumed that the skills a student brings from school, or even from the first year of university, are sufficient to carry them through their degree. Skills such as, task management, working with others, and critical thinking need to be fine-tuned and extended as students move from one level to another.

Globally, universities and colleges are giving far more attention to preparatory support for prospective students and to developing study skills once a student is on a programme. In some countries, there is a growing emphasis, too, on "employability skills," from soft skills such as communication, creativity, and working collaboratively to new attributes sought by employers, including business acumen, cross-cultural sensitivity, and enterprise. In addition, each institution tends to identify a range of skills and qualities that it wants to see embodied by its graduates.

One of the challenges is articulating what is meant by study skills in this changing environment. This has significance for students when trying to make sense of long lists of skills that they are expected to accumulate during their time in higher education. It also has a bearing on who teaches and supports study skills. In some colleges and universities this falls to study skills specialists; in others, it may be allocated to teaching staff. In each case, different approaches are used to make sense of the learning experience.

From the students' perspective, it helps to organize study skills into a few, relatively easy-to-remember categories. In the latest version of *The Study Skills Handbook*, I suggest using four basic categories:

1 Self   2 Academic   3 People   4 Task

The starting place for students is being able to manage themselves within a new learning environment with confidence and resilience. They need to understand the rationale for, and benefits of, independent study and the kinds of challenges that they will be set. This involves organizing their time, coping with deadlines, and recognizing what it means to take charge of their own learning. It also includes metacognitive skills in reflecting on how they think, learn, and manage themselves for study.

Academic skills consist of such skills as the core research skills (finding, recording, and using information), thinking skills (critical thinking skills, creative problem-solving, and synthesis); understanding academic conventions (the nature and integrity of academic study), and writing skills.

People skills are increasingly important as collaborative study becomes a feature of higher education. These include such skills as giving and receiving criticism, supporting others without cheating, group project work, and playing an active role in group sessions. These can be an especial challenge for international students who may be used to different kinds of learning interactions.

Task management skills within this learning context include such skills as meeting given requirements and using appropriate protocols and project management in order to achieve a given academic task such as writing an essay or report, undertaking research, conducting an experiment, or solving a problem.

An additional value of this framework is that the basic shell can be easily adapted to other contexts, such as employability. The "Self / People / Tasks" model is one that I used, for example within *Skills for Success: Personal Development and Employability (2010)*.

Stella Cottrell is Director for Lifelong Learning at the University of Leeds, UK. She is author of the bestselling *The Study Skills Handbook, The Palgrave Student Planner, The Exam Skills Handbook, Critical Thinking Skills, Study Skills Connected*, and *Skills for Success*, all published by Palgrave Macmillan.

Reference
Hurley, J. (1994), Supporting Learning (Bristol: The Staff College and Learning Partners).

Teaching academic vocabulary by Pete Sharma

It has been estimated that in an academic text, a quarter of the words are either "academic vocabulary" or "technical vocabulary." What is "academic vocabulary"? The term includes:

- concepts, such as *research*
- actions, such as *classifying* and *defining*
- nouns, such as *sources* and *references*
- collocations, such as *reading list*, and
- reporting, language such as *argue*.

Academic vocabulary is used across all disciplines. This essay will describe a range of activities for teaching academic vocabulary.

Students meet and practice new vocabulary in every kind of lesson, and especially in reading and listening lessons. In a listening lesson, you may pre-teach key vocabulary before students do the listening task. Similarly, in a reading lesson, you can pre-teach specific words to make the text easier to read. Throughout the *Skillful* Students' Book, there are "Vocabulary skill" boxes, and "Academic keyword" boxes which signal important words.

Giving presentations provides opportunities for students to use and practice new vocabulary, and for you to provide feedback on their pronunciation. Similarly, writing essays allows learners to produce the new words they have learnt in context.

During the course, you will not only present and practice vocabulary but also give advice on effective learning strategies. Explore the different ways students can record the new vocabulary they meet on the course. Many students merely jot down a word and write a translation next to it, so it is helpful to present alternatives, such as creating "word trees." Have students work together to create mind-maps on relevant topics, as we remember words when we meet them in concept groups. The *Skillful* Teacher's Book includes several ideas for using a vocabulary notebook. Point out that many words have a standard meaning and an academic meaning. Give examples: references; argument.

Students frequently start their academic course over-using their bilingual dictionary. They benefit from a lesson or lessons exploring the pros and cons of using a monolingual, English-English dictionary. A good way to start a dictionary lesson is to do a quiz to show some useful dictionary features in the dictionary. Part of a lesson can be spent introducing learners to electronic dictionaries, which allow students to listen to new words. You can demonstrate a CD-ROM and web-based dictionary using a data projector.

There are several important features of academic vocabulary that you will wish to focus on during the course. It is useful to provide practice on prefixes and suffixes, since noticing patterns in the language can help learners work out the meaning of new words. Also, focus on "collocation" or "word partnerships." Before students read a text, you can select some key collocations, write them on cards, and get students to match them. Students can then scan the text and highlight these collocations before moving to more intensive reading practice. There are several language exercises on prefixes, suffixes, and collocations in *Skillful* and the Teacher's Book also contains sets of photocopiable cards which can be used in many ways, as warmers for example, or for reviewing lexis.

There is no need to develop a new methodology for teaching academic vocabulary. Good practice involves students meeting new words in context, practicing them in speaking and writing, and recycling them in a variety of ways. Working through the units and different levels of *Skillful* will enable students to practice and review academic vocabulary systematically.

Pete Sharma is an associate Lecturer at Oxford Brookes University, UK. He has written books on technology in language teaching, and is co-author of *Blended Learning* (Macmillan: 2007) and *400 Ideas for Interactive Whiteboards* (Macmillan: 2010).

Educational culture by Stacey H. Hughes

Most language teachers have an understanding of culture and the differences that can arise in culturally diverse situations. By extension, when it comes to the classroom, it is important to consider the mix of the culture that our students bring into the classroom, that teachers bring into it, and the cultural expectations of the institution itself. Each culture has its own expectations of the role of the teacher, the students, the material, and the aim of education. Unmet expectations can lead to frustration on the part of the teacher, and poor learning or lack of achievement and dwindling motivation on the part of the learners. It is therefore important to be acutely aware of behavioral and learning expectations.

What is good learning? What is good teaching?

Every educational setting has an idea of what good education means. Teachers and students tend to assume that they share ideas about how to teach and how to learn, or about what good teaching and learning is. However, concepts of "good student" and "good teacher" vary widely from culture to culture. Consequently, students attending university in a foreign country for the first time often have to go through a difficult adjustment period as they learn to adapt to their new educational culture. There are a number of areas that students will need to adjust to. These include differences in teaching style and methodology, differences in what is expected of students in terms of output and behavior, and differences in the expectation of the university itself.

Teacher / student roles and expectations

So, how do educational expectations vary across cultures? Firstly, teacher and student roles and expectations vary widely. For example, teachers in many East Asian classrooms expect their students to be active listeners, and what it means to be a good student is to listen carefully and reflect on the knowledge the teacher is imparting. In other words, they expect students to master the knowledge and skills that they and the coursebook impart. Similarly in many Middle Eastern cultures, the teacher expects the students to memorize what they present. By contrast, in the West, students are expected to ask questions and think critically. Accepting without question is not necessarily a sign of good learning. As to student expectations, in many countries, students expect the teacher to be the authority figure who knows all the answers, or even a moral leader. This expectation can contrast sharply with a culture such as that of the U.K. where teachers are not necessarily expected to have all the answers.

Classroom organization and methodology

Classroom organization and teaching or methodological style can vary as well. In U.K. university classrooms, for example, the atmosphere tends to be less formal, with teachers using humor, emphasizing student participation and debate, and even encouraging students to disagree with them. Active participation is seen as evidence of learning. Teachers also feel students should reflect on their own work and be able to critique the work of their peers. Desks may be arranged in groups or in a semi-circle to facilitate interaction. These differences can feel quite strange to students who are used to a more formal classroom setting and who would not expect importance to be placed on their personal views. While group assignments may be given in Asian and Middle Eastern cultures as well, the classroom setting may tend to be more lecture-orientated.

In conclusion, it is clear that teachers and students bring educational expectations with them into the classroom and that critical thinking, evaluation, reflection, discussion, and learner autonomy are important elements. However, it may be difficult for teachers to know how to bridge the gap between themselves, the students, and the methodology. What is needed firstly is for teachers to be aware of their own underlying cultural expectations and how these are manifested in their teaching practice. They then need to consider whether this classroom practice incorporates the kinds of skills that will help students reach their educational potential in the twenty-first century. And finally, teachers need to spend class time on learner training. It is important for teachers and students to spend this time discussing teaching and learning expectations and roles. Students will most likely not have an awareness of their own educational expectations or that there are any other cultures of education. Teachers need to give a rationale for the skills necessary for EAP and anticipate such questions as, "Why are we doing this?" Stating aims may not be enough. Teachers need to think of how those aims are perceived at the cultural level and help students acculturate to the expectations and requirements of the educational culture they are in.

Stacey Hughes is a lecturer at Oxford Brookes University. Her main interests in ELT are learner engagement, active learning, critical thinking, and intercultural issues.

Integrating reading and writing skills by David Bohlke

The connection between reading and writing may seem obvious. Both use the written form, but their connection goes much deeper than that. Today, these two skills are still at times taught separately, but it is actually difficult to separate them.

What do we do when we read and write? Writing is an active process. There is no writing unless we create it. Reading, however, has traditionally been seen as more passive. But this view is changing. Deriving meaning from reading relies on the interaction between the writer, text, and reader. This, along with context, determines what a particular text may mean to any particular reader.

Reading can be used to improve performance on a writing task. To appreciate good writing, it is important for learners to see how language works in different ways. A reading can also provide new, inspiring ideas for a writing assignment. This exposure to authentic language in a natural context is highly beneficial to writers. The text can also act as a model for a specific writing genre showing correct register, organization structure, and tone.

Writing can be used to better understand reading. When we read, actions such as highlighting, taking notes or writing summaries encourage readers to be more active. By making the comprehension of the text more "visible," this may help the reader remember key points. It also shows that the author's voice is not necessarily the last word on the subject.

The following tips can enhance your learners' ability in both skills.

1 Draw on what you know Good readers activate background knowledge when they engage with a text. By tapping into this, they make important connections to the new information encountered in a text. Good writers also activate prior knowledge through brainstorming activities.

2 Vary your sentences Good readers know good writing when they see it. They are constantly applying their knowledge of grammar to build comprehension of a text. Good writers also use a variety of sentence patterns to engage and entertain the reader.

3 Build vocabulary Good readers build vocabulary through continued reading. Possessing a rich vocabulary allows readers to read with less effort and with a deeper understanding. Good writers use clear, precise words to state exactly what they mean and are competent users of both a dictionary and a thesaurus.

4 Understand coherence Coherence is the unity created among the various ideas, sentences, and paragraphs of a text. Good readers can recognize a coherent text through the author's use of transition words, parallel structure, and sense of organization. Good writers stay on topic and do not offer irrelevant details that distract or confuse the reader.

5 Identify your audience Good readers feel a connection with the text, and by extension, its writer. They often imagine the writer is speaking directly to them. Good writers always consider their audience. They anticipate the readers' response and carry on an internal dialogue with them as they write.

6 Know your genres Each genre has its own unique characteristics, style, and purpose. Good readers use this knowledge to help them identify text type, predict content, follow an argument, and draw conclusions. Good writers are familiar with different genres and use knowledge of their structural characteristics to produce appropriate texts.

7 Develop critical thinking Good readers do not just decode a text and take away its literal meaning. They understand what a text means, rather than just what it says or does. This involves considering, analyzing, evaluating, and inferring to find a deeper understanding of a text. Good critical writers are also good critical readers. They assess and interpret key information and draw conclusions from them.

Connecting reading and writing in the classroom is an important step toward reinforcing learning in both skill areas. Because academic success depends on interacting with a text in multiple ways, development in both is essential.

David Bohlke has 25 years of experience as a teacher, trainer, program director, editor, and materials developer. He has taught in Japan, Korea, Saudi Arabia, and Morocco, and has conducted multiple teacher-training workshops around the world.

UNIT 1 CHARACTER

Reading	Previewing
	Using pronouns
Vocabulary	Using examples to find meaning
Writing	Writing topic sentences
Grammar	The simple present tense

Discussion point

Ask students to look at the pictures on page 7 and answer these questions: *What are some of the emotions he is feeling? Which man would you like to meet / not like to meet? Why? Why do you think there are so many pictures of him?*

Try to get students to guess the meaning of the word *character* from context clues, e.g. ask: *What do the pictures show about his personality, or character? Which picture shows he has a bad personality, or character? Which shows good personality, or character?*

EXTENSION ACTIVITY

If you have time, and a creative class, you could stage a caption contest. Assign a picture to a pair of students. Ask them to draw a speech or thinking bubble and write what the man is saying or thinking.

Ask students to discuss the questions with a partner, using the sentence frames to help them get started. Photocopy and cut out the unit 1 *Useful language* page to provide some extra support. After students have discussed the three questions, have them share their answers with the class.

Vocabulary preview

For this exercise, students should avoid using dictionaries, especially bilingual ones, and should guess the meaning of the words in bold from the context of the sentence. A good monolingual dictionary such as the *Macmillan Essential Dictionary* could be used to check answers if needed, or to check pronunciation. Make sure students know the correct pronunciation of the words in bold. Ask them to underline the stressed syllable in each word.

It is a good idea to encourage students to keep a vocabulary notebook to note down words that they learn from each unit. Rather than simply recording the word in English and the translation, encourage them to record words in a way that will help them use them in the future. They should record the pronunciation, part of speech (noun, verb, etc.), and the meaning or synonym / antonym. They could also add any collocations and example sentences. How they

organize the notebook is up to them: alphabetically, by date, or by topic. The notebooks can be used in future vocabulary revision activities.

ANSWERS
1 d   2 e   3 a   4 b   5 c   6 j   7 f   8 g
9 h   10 i

READING 1   Are you a natural leader?

Word count 211

Background information

The people pictured represent leaders from a range of fields. Though leadership qualities may differ from one context to another, there may be some qualities that all leaders may possess.

Martin Luther King, Jr.—civil rights leader in the U.S.A.; fought for equal rights for black Americans; received the Nobel Peace Prize and gave the money to the civil rights movement; assassinated

Hilary Clinton—67th U.S. secretary of state; former First Lady married to President Clinton; advocate and supporter of a state health care plan—especially for children—and other child protection acts

Marie Curie—Polish physicist and chemist who did research on radioactivity; discovered polonium and radium; won two Nobel Peace Prizes; first woman to win a Nobel Peace Prize; founded *Institut Curie* for medical research

Ban Ki-moon—Korean diplomat; 8th Secretary General of the UN; his efforts for reform include UN peace-keeping missions and curbing greenhouse emissions; has received many awards and honors

Mark Zuckerberg—software developer, co-creator, and CEO of Facebook; has been named in the top 100 most influential people in the world and as Person of the Year in 2012 *Time Magazine*; one of the world's youngest billionaires

J.K. Rowling—novelist; movie producer; author of the *Harry Potter* series who went from being a divorced, jobless mother to authoring the number one best-selling book series in history; philanthropic supporter of several charities

Before you read

1 Check students are able to pronounce the words in the *Qualities* box. Ask them to discuss the questions in pairs, using the sentence frames to help them. Provide a model if necessary.

Exam tip

Previewing is an important reading skill because it helps readers build a context in their mind of what they are going to read. Previewing will also help students read more quickly and more effectively, and is a useful skill for students to use in exams.

2 Direct students' attention to the *Previewing* box and ask them to read it silently for two minutes. Check students understanding of previewing by asking them: *What do you need to look at before you read a text? What three (or more) things can you learn about a text before you actually read it? Why do you think it is important to preview a text? When you read in your own language, do you use any previewing strategies?* Then ask the students to discuss the questions with a partner.

Global reading

Ask students to read the text and check their ideas.

ANSWER

It's a survey or questionnaire you would find in a magazine. You would complete the survey to find out if you were a natural leader.

Close reading

1 Ask students to read the article and do the exercise. When they have finished, ask individual students to share some of their ideas.

2 Ask students to find the statements in the survey that are similar to the statements in exercise 2. Check the answers with the class.

ANSWERS

a 12   b 17   c 1   d 8   e 14   f 18

3 Ask students to find the statements in the survey that are the opposite to the statements in exercise 3. Check the answers with the class.

ANSWERS

a 20   b 2   c 7   d 9   e 11   f 13

EXTENSION ACTIVITY

Divide your class into two groups and have one group do exercise 2 and the other do exercise 3. They can then test each other.

Direct students' attention to the *Academic keywords* box. These are used to show items of crucial academic vocabulary from the texts and are very important for developing students' receptive academic vocabulary store. Make sure they can pronounce the words and tell them to add them to their vocabulary notebooks.

Developing critical thinking

SUPPORTING CRITICAL THINKING

Critical thinking is about questioning claims and assumptions. It involves using evidence, context, one's own experience, the source of the information, etc. to reflect on and evaluate an idea. It is a key academic skill and, arguably, an important life skill. Instead of accepting an argument or claim as it is, students need to decide if it is true or valid. Critical thinking is increasingly important as more and more information can be found on the web.

Critical thinking can be extended to outside of class. Ask students to keep a journal in which they respond to the critical thinking questions in writing. These journals would not be corrected for grammar, but should encourage the free flow of ideas. They could be collected at regular intervals for checking and response.

The questions in this section are designed to encourage students to think about the text more deeply. Encourage students to discuss the questions together as each individual will bring a different experience to the discussion. Encourage students to give their opinion and to listen carefully to other students' opinions and ideas. Their discussions should broaden their perspectives. Be sure to direct students to the sentence frames and *Faults* box which will help them in their discussion.

Cultural awareness

What makes a good leader can vary according to culture. For example, in a collectivist culture, a good leader might be someone who best represents the group, while in an individualistic culture, a good leader may be someone who has shown they can surmount obstacles on their own. Leaders in high power distance societies may be very authoritarian, paternalistic, and older, while in low power distance societies they may be quite young, egalitarian, and part of the team. Ask students to describe some of the qualities that leaders in their culture possess.

If the survey in the Student's Book does not fit the students' definition of a good leader, then they could be asked to write a similar survey for their country.

Students could be asked to make a poster describing good leadership qualities appropriate to their country or cultural context.

Students could be asked to research a leader they admire and list the qualities that make them a good leader. This could be done as a poster or writing task.

READING 2 The hero within

Word count 463

Before you read

Background information

The idea of a superhero is not a new one. In eighth century western literature, for example, Beowulf was cast as a "super human" who battled and defeated an evil monster no others could defeat. In the mid twentieth century, comic book superheroes such as Superman and the Fantastic Four were introduced. Superheroes are not just American. China's include Atom and Radioactive man; Japan, Tako Samara and Naiad; and Korea has Mystek. Islamic superheroes include characters from The 99 such as Jabbar the Powerful and Sami the Listener.

Comic books featuring superheroes are popular and collectible—some issues have been sold for thousands of dollars. Examples of comics include Marvel, DC Comics, Action Comics, The 99, Doujinshi, and Manga. There are also many movies about superheroes: *Spider-Man, Hulk, X-Men, Fantastic Four Iron Man*, and recently, *The Avengers*. Interestingly, the first ever comic book, *kibyōshi*, was published in Japan in 1775.

This is a good place to use the video resource *What makes a good hero?* It is located in the Video resources section of the Digibook. Alternatively, remind the students about the video resource so they can do this at home.

1 After students have discussed the questions with a partner, have them share their ideas with the class.

2 Remind students of the previewing skill that they learned in the previous section. Ask them to look at the picture and title on page 11 and predict what the article is going to be about.

ANSWERS
The article is about what makes a superhero.

Global reading

For the first reading, set a time limit of three minutes so that students read quickly to find the seven superhero characteristics. At this stage, deter students from referring to dictionaries.

ANSWERS
1 super-human powers	5 super-villain
2 secret identity	6 backstory
3 colorful costume	7 weakness
4 strong moral code	

Close reading

1 This exercise requires students to understand what they have read because the sentences are not exactly the same as in the original text. Set a time limit of five minutes for the exercise. At this stage, students could be permitted to use their *Macmillan Essential Dictionary* if necessary, but they should not look up every word. The *Using examples to find meaning* section on page 12 focuses on using context clues to discover a word's meaning. If appropriate, this section could be introduced before asking students to do this exercise.

POSSIBLE ANSWERS
1 rebirth	5 uninteresting
2 identity	6 human nature
3 strong moral code	7 crime and war
4 good and evil	8 perfect

2 Students will recognize pronouns, but may not know what they are called. Provide some examples (*he / she / they / it*) and elicit the word *pronoun*. Ask students why we use pronouns and let them check to see if they were correct by reading the *Using pronouns* box. After they have read it, ask students what an *antecedent* is. You may need to give an example, e.g.

The waiters in the restaurant were very rude. They said I had to leave.

(*The waiters* is the antecedent.)

Ask students to do the exercise, then check the answers with the class.

ANSWERS
1 a all superheroes	b the law
2 a a weakness	b a superhero
3 a our own fears	b our own fears

Draw students' attention to the words in the *Academic keywords* box and make sure they can pronounce them. Ask the students to add them to their vocabulary notebooks. You might need to introduce some collocations to help students use the words correctly, e.g. *overcome* a problem, **moral** code, code of *conduct*.

Developing critical thinking

SUPPORTING CRITICAL THINKING

In exercise 2 of this section, students are required to synthesize and evaluate issues from both reading texts in the unit. Drawing on more than one source for comment is a key academic skill, so encourage students to think about the issues that arose from both texts. If your students have lower level speaking skills, you could ask them to choose one question from each exercise to discuss.

1 Ask students to discuss the questions in groups. When they have finished, ask them to share their ideas with the whole class.

2 Remind students of the text *Are you a natural leader?* Ask them if they think there is a connection between this text and *The hero within*. Then ask them to discuss the questions in groups. Draw their attention to the *Think about* box to give them ideas.

Vocabulary skill

Students often get stuck while reading when they encounter a word they don't know. By the time they have looked up the word and possibly translated it into their language, they have lost the thread of what they were reading and can quickly become frustrated. To become proficient readers, students need to try to use context clues to help them figure out the word. This skill speeds up reading time and aids comprehension.

This section could be done prior to the close reading activity on page 10 if appropriate.

Ask students what they do when they see a word they don't know while they are reading. Ask them if they think it's possible to understand some words without looking them up. If so, how? Write an example on the board, e.g. *Spider-Man can catch villains in his **web**, just like a spider catches flies.* Ask students if they can guess what a *web* is from the context (spiders / catching flies). Ask students to read the *Using explanations to find meaning* box on page 32 to find out another way they can discover the meaning of new words. Check their comprehension, then ask them to complete the exercises.

1 Ask students to do the exercise individually, then check the answers with the class.

ANSWERS
1 b   2 b   3 a

2 Ask students to do the exercise individually, then check the answers with the class.

ANSWERS
1 a   2 b   3 b

WRITING Describing a hero

Writing skill

Cultural awareness

What is considered good paragraph structure differs from one culture to another. In East Asian cultures, students are taught to write around and around the main idea, which is then stated at the end in a delayed statement of purpose. People from Middle Eastern countries write in a parallel structure. Romance language and Slavic speakers follow a pattern of frequent digressions from the main point. In academic English, paragraphs tend to be linear, progressing from a broad main idea to more specific supporting details. Students used to a different writing convention may have trouble with the structure of an academic English paragraph. The following exercises are designed to help students identify what a topic sentence is and where it may be found. They also give students practice in recognizing and writing topic sentences.

1 Lead into the idea of writing topic sentences by discussing what a topic is. Ask students to tell you the broad topic of a recently-read book or article or a recently-seen TV show. Then direct students to read the *Writing topic sentences* box. When they have finished, ask them to do the exercise. Then check the answers with the class.

ANSWERS
1 T   2 F   3 T   4 F   5 F

2 Tell students to underline the topic sentence in each paragraph. When they have finished, ask them to say what it is that make them the "topic sentences." Create a list of criteria on the board to be used in the next exercises. For example, *a topic sentence is a broad statement; it may be followed by examples; a topic sentence introduces the paragraph; it may be a fact that is supported by evidence afterwards,* etc.

ANSWERS

Paragraph 1: What makes a superhero, and why are they likely not going anywhere soon?

Paragraph 2: Nearly all fictional superheroes have super-human powers.

Paragraph 3: A secret identity helps protect the superhero's family and friends.

Paragraph 4: A colorful costume, such as Spider-Man's web design or Captain America's U.S. flag costume, helps the public recognize the superhero, and at the same time it hides his or her identity.

Paragraph 5: All superheroes are honest and possess a strong moral code.

Paragraph 6: Superheroes would not exist without the super-villain.

Paragraph 7: The backstory tells how the superhero actually became the superhero we know.

Paragraph 8: A weakness can make a superhero helpless.

Paragraph 9: The superhero is perhaps not so different from us.

3 Ask the students to circle the topic sentences, then check the answers with the class.

ANSWERS

1 b   2 b   3 b

4 This exercise could be done in pairs or individually. Ask students to write their topic sentences on large slips of paper that can be displayed around the room, or onto overhead transparencies that can be projected. As a class, decide which sentences fit the criteria for topic sentences brainstormed in exercise 2.

Grammar

Refer students to the information in the *Grammar* box. Note that in academic writing, contractions (e.g. *don't* and *doesn't*) are not used. Students need to be made aware of this important difference from less formal writing genres.

1 Ask the students to complete the sentences with the correct form of the verbs in the box, then check the answers with the class.

ANSWERS

1 think	4 know
2 has	5 see
3 like	6 belong

2 Ask students to work individually to rewrite the sentences in exercise 1, then check the answers with the class.

ANSWERS

1 I do not think superhero stories are just for kids.
2 My brother does not have a lot of comic books.
3 My friends and I do not like the X-Men.
4 I do not know the plots of most superhero stories.
5 Our teachers do not see hero qualities in us.
6 These comic books do not belong to my cousin.

WRITING TASK

Before asking students to read the model paragraph, do a quick introduction of the idea of everyday heroes by asking students what the difference is between a hero and a superhero. Ask them if they know any heroes. Brainstorm some quick ideas about what might make an everyday hero. Then, ask them to read the paragraph and do the task.

ANSWERS

Everyone has a hero. I think that everyday heroes like police officers and firefighters are true heroes. My hero is my Uncle Manuel. He works as a police officer. I really respect him. He protects our city and keeps us safe. He works long and difficult hours. For example, he often works from 11:00 p.m. to 7:00 a.m. He has to cope with a stressful and difficult job, but he never complains. He is a very honest man. He does not make much money. He does this work because he cares about people. He wants to help them and contribute something to our city. People sometimes thank him. I want more people to do that. We need to appreciate these everyday heroes more.

Exam tip

The five stages in the writing section are important in developing students' ability to plan, write, and review their work. Brainstorming using a word map is a good way for students to generate ideas. Planning is the next crucial step in the writing process and will lead to a more coherent paragraph. Students may try to skip planning stages in an exam situation because they think that they don't have time for it. However, they need to learn that these steps are crucial in creating well-organized, thoughtful writing. Similarly, students need to understand that going back to check their work will also lead to a better paragraph. Students will find it hard to review their own work, but asking them to assess their work with the checklist, for example, will give them focus on what to look for.

Brainstorm, plan, and write

Students should aim to write 100–120 words on the topic of *My hero*, using the paragraph on page 15 as a model if needed. If students cannot think of a personal everyday hero, they could invent one or think of everyday heroes in a wider context. Encourage them to use the word map to brainstorm and plan their paragraph. Remind them to write a topic sentence before beginning their paragraph.

Share, rewrite, and edit

Have the students exchange their paragraphs with a partner. Sharing work with a partner may be a new experience for students and may take them some time to get comfortable with. They may think that comments from peers are less valuable than teacher feedback or may feel that they have little authority to comment on other students' writing. However, peer review is important in developing learner autonomy and moving away from dependence on the teacher. It is worth spending some time to set this up and establish rules for reviewing each other's work. Using the checklist on page 109 of the Student's Book can help peer reviewers know what to look for when evaluating each other's paragraphs. Students need not check each other's grammar, but can make comments about structure and can ask questions about content.

Rewriting and editing are also very important steps which students may not be accustomed to. Encourage them to check their tenses and take their peer's comments into consideration when rewriting.

Use the photocopiable unit assignment checklist on page 88 to assess the students' paragraphs.

Extra research task

Ask students to research an organization which could be classed as "heroic" or as doing heroic work. Examples might include charitable organizations such as Medicins sans Frontiers or Oxfam. Students could then write a paragraph describing why they think the organization is "heroic."

STUDY SKILLS Setting up a study space

Background information

Often students do not know how to study. The *Study skills* sections focus on different ways that students can become better at studying. This section helps guide students towards setting up an appropriate study space by highlighting some of the things that make a study space ineffective. Poor study space can lead to students being distracted, or even falling asleep. Often students say that they study better with the TV or radio on. Research has shown that this is not necessarily true, though certain types of classical music have been shown to boost brain activity. Even good students can benefit from improved study skills.

Getting started

Ask the students to discuss the questions with a partner. Monitor the activity and elicit feedback.

Scenario

Ask students to do this exercise with a partner. Elicit whole-class feedback from one pair and check to see if the rest of the class agrees.

POSSIBLE ANSWER
Hamid has a large workspace and can spread out his books. However, he shouldn't lie on his bed to work or have the TV on. He should ask his brother not to come in when he is studying.

Consider it

After pairs have discussed the tips, have a whole-class check of the students' ideas. Students may have other ideas to contribute to this list. Ask students to use the list to set up their study space at home.

Over to you

Ask students to discuss the questions with a partner. Monitor the activity and elicit feedback.

UNIT 2 TIME

Reading	Identifying the author's purpose Skimming
Vocabulary	Organizing new words: nouns and verbs
Writing	Understanding sentence patterns
Grammar	Verbs followed by infinitives and gerunds

Discussion point

Ask students how the picture on page 17 relates to the topic of the unit. Hopefully they will be able to identify the picture as the inner workings of a clock. You could initiate a quick class discussion about clocks and watches. Ask: *How many people are wearing a watch? How many people have an alarm clock? What other ways do you check the time?* Check that students know the difference between a watch and a clock. Ask the students to discuss the questions with a partner, using the sentence frames to help them get started. Photocopy and cut out the unit 2 *Useful language* page to provide some extra support. After students have discussed the three questions, have them share their answers with the class.

EXTENSION ACTIVITY

Ask students to interview several students and record their answers. Record these on the board as a class poll.

Vocabulary preview

Exam tip

In this task, students have to try to understand the meaning of the words in bold from context. Using context clues is an important reading skill that students need to learn in order to become proficient readers. It is also an important exam skill because students will not be able to use dictionaries during exams. Students can get too dependent on dictionaries and may tend to look up every word that they do not understand. This is unnecessary because it is possible to understand a text without knowing every word (we do it in our own language all the time). It also slows down their reading and makes it ineffective. In order to build students' tolerance for some ambiguity and ability to understand the meaning of a text without understanding every word, deter students from using their dictionaries when doing the readings in class. At first, you may need to point out clues that can help them determine the meaning.

Ask students to work individually or with a partner to do this activity. When they have finished, do a quick whole-class check.

ANSWERS

1 a   2 a   3 b   4 a   5 a   6 a   7 b

READING 1 A matter of time

Word count 443

Background information

Blog (n) (v): *web + log = blog*

A blog is a kind of journal that is published on the web. It is a place for people to write about anything they wish and to invite other people to read and comment on what has been written. Blogs may deal with one subject and be a virtual space in which a group discusses that subject, or they may be a personal space for someone to express ideas. Blogs may also be used as promotion tools for goods and services. Blogs can contain text, pictures, links, video, audio, and music, and entries in the blog are called "posts." Blogging is hugely popular and is a form of social networking.

Before you read

Ask students if they know what a blog is and show them an example of a blog, if you have access to the Internet. Ask them where blogs can be found (on the Internet) and what kinds of blogs there are. Ask them to look at the *Types of blog* box to get some ideas. There are several sites where it is possible to set up a free blog, e.g. www.blogger.com is one such site.

1 Ask students to discuss the questions with a partner or in groups. Remind them to refer to the ideas in the *Types of blog* box. Then elicit whole-class feedback.

2 Have students focus on the title A *matter of time* and the picture on page 19 for a few seconds. After students have discussed the questions with a partner, ask them to share their ideas with the whole class.

ANSWERS

1 It's about time management.
2 It represents the expression "time flies." In other words, it shows that time passes quickly.

Cultural awareness

Time is extremely important in some cultures and less important in others. In monochronic time cultures (such as the U.S., U.K., Germany, Switzerland, and Scandinavia), punctuality is important because time is seen as valuable. People in these cultures like schedules and fixed appointments. Time is seen as something that can be spent, saved, and wasted. On the other hand, in polychronic time cultures (such as Mediterranean countries), more emphasis is placed on interactions between people than in holding to schedules. Time is not very important, and this is evident in the unimportance attached to punctuality. It is more important to speak with a friend than to be on time for class, for example. When monochronic and polychronic time cultures have to work together, culture clashes can happen.

You could discuss the importance of time in students' cultures by introducing them to some common time expressions (possibly as a matching exercise) and seeing which ones they most identify with. Some examples are: *Time is money* (= time is valuable), *spend time with someone, killing time* (= wasting time), *have a good time, to buy time, take your time* (= go slowly), *don't waste time, find the time* (to do something important), *the time of your life, run out of time, good timing*. For more examples, search for *time idioms*.

Global reading

Give students three minutes to scan the article quickly and underline the seven tips. Avoid dictionary use. Then check the answers with the class.

> **ANSWERS**
> 1 Write it down
> 2 Prioritize
> 3 Don't skip the breaks
> 4 One thing at a time
> 5 Schedule email time
> 6 Choose to say "no"
> 7 Keep a goal journal

Close reading

1 In this exercise students need to be able to understand the tips and apply them to different people. When students have finished the exercise, check the answers with the class.

> **ANSWERS**
> a 5   b 3   c 4   d 6   e 1   f 7   g 2

2 Ask the students who they think writes blogs and why. There may be many different reasons. Ask them to read the *Identifying the author's purpose* box. Then check comprehension by asking: *What purposes might a writer have for writing? Why do we need to know why someone writes something?* Ask students to check the author's main purpose, then check the answer with the class.

> **ANSWER**
> 1 inform

Exam tip

Identifying the author's purpose is an important academic (critical thinking) skill to build, and it is one of the task types on the IELTS exam. Knowing why an author writes something helps us make judgments about the text and the views in the text.

You may also want students to find the words from the *Academic keywords* box in the text and check that they know the meaning and pronunciation. Then they can add these to their vocabulary notebook. If students are using the Digibook, tell them that they can click on the icon next to the *Academic keywords* box to reveal definitions and example sentences for each word.

Developing critical thinking

SUPPORTING CRITICAL THINKING

Question 1 asks students to give their opinion and then give reasons for it. Evaluating a text and then giving reasons to support their opinions prepares students for more advanced activities in which they have to support opinions with evidence or examples.

Critical thinking can be extended to outside of the classroom. Ask students to keep a journal in which they respond to the critical thinking questions in writing. These journals would not be corrected for grammar, but should encourage the free flow of ideas. They could be collected at regular intervals for checking and response.

Ask students to give their views and then give reasons for them. Giving reasons for views is an important evaluation skill. Encourage them to use the words in the *Useful words* box when discussing question 3. When the students have finished discussing in groups, ask them to share their ideas with the class.

Extra research task

Why not set up a class blog? There are lots of how-to blog sites on the web (search for *blog tutorial* or *how to blog*).

READING 2 What time is it?

Word count 418

Background information

Since 1884, all time zones are measured from the Greenwich (pronounced /'grenɪtʃ/) Meridian Line at the Royal Observatory in Greenwich, England. This is referred to as *Greenwich Mean Time* (GMT). Though many countries change the times in the spring and fall (in spring the clocks go forward, and in fall they go back), GMT stays the same year around. GMT is also known as *Zulu Time* by the Navy and in civil aviation. The term *Coordinated Universal Time* (UTC) is also common and is a more accurate measure because it takes the Earth's rotation into consideration.

Before you read

You could lead in to this section simply by asking students what time it is. You may need to pre-teach *accurate* (exact, precise, correct). After the students have done the experiments with a partner, ask them to share their ideas with the whole class. As a follow-up to the experiments, you could find out how many people still wear a watch and how accurate the students' timekeeping devices are. You could ask students to write down the time on their watch or phone, and compare answers. Ask: *Does everyone have the same time?* Ask students to tell you how to find out the *exact* time (e.g. go to www.atomicclock.org.uk).

Exam tip

Skimming is helpful in exams as there is not always enough time to read the text slowly and carefully. You could introduce this section by asking students if they read different texts in different ways. For example, ask students to compare how they read the football results or a recipe to how they might read a novel. Students need to be aware that it is OK to read quickly in English to get a general idea without understanding every word. One way to get students to stop looking up every word is to get them to cross out any word they don't know and then tell you what the general meaning is.

Global reading

Ask the students to read the *Skimming* box, then ask questions to check their comprehension, e.g. *Is skimming quick reading or intensive reading? Is it reading for detail or for the main idea? Do you have to understand every word? What things other than the reading itself can help you get a general idea?*

Ask students to skim the text, then check what it is about. Students may need to be pre-taught the following vocabulary: *straightforward* (easy), *punctual* (on time).

ANSWER

2 A history of clocks

Close reading

1   Ask students to do the exercise individually, then check the answers with the class. As an extension to exercise 1, ask students to draw or describe how each of the clocks works, based on their reading of the text. They could do this as a group activity, with each group being given a different clock to draw and label or describe, and then present. Encourage them to use their own words.

ANSWERS

1 c   2 e   3 a   4 d   5 b   6 f

2   Ask students to write answers to the questions, then check the answers with the class.

ANSWERS

1 It was smaller.
2 It was impossible to tell time on cloudy days or at night.
3 They were used in Egypt, the Middle East, and China.
4 Clocks began to be more accurate in the thirteenth century.
5 Springs improved their accuracy.
6 People started to rely on clocks to run businesses after 1927, when the quartz clock was developed.

Developing critical thinking

1   This exercise requires that students think laterally. They can think of other timekeeping devices or think of other ways of measuring time. For example, we measure a day from when the sun rises to when it sets. You could ask groups to prepare their answers to question 1 on a large piece of paper or overhead transparency (OHT) that they can show to the rest of the class. They could then present their views to either the rest of the class or to another group, depending on class size.

Be sure to refer students to the *Academic keywords* box and the useful language in the *Think about* box, ensuring that they know how to pronounce the terms. If using the Digibook, you can expand the box here to see more information about each term. Then they can add these to their vocabulary notebooks.

2   Remind students of the text *A matter of time*. Ask them if they think there is a connection between this text and *What time is it?* Then ask them to discuss the questions in groups. Remind them to refer to the *Think about* box. These questions are key study skills questions that could be exploited

further. You might ask students to follow up their discussion on a class blog, or as a journal assignment, or in a reflective paragraph. Effective time management skills are discussed further in the *Study skills* section in unit 5.

Vocabulary skill

Begin by checking that students understand the term *parts of speech* by asking them to identify different parts of speech (nouns, verbs, adjectives, adverbs, articles, pronouns). Ask them to read the *Organizing new words: nouns and verbs* box, and then check comprehension by asking them to identify some nouns and verbs from the unit. Ask: *Is digital clock a noun or a verb? Is develop a noun or a verb?*

At this point, you might also point out that certain words can be either a noun or a verb, depending on the context, e.g. *a blog / to blog; a clock / to clock; a watch / to watch.* The key here is context. Some of the words in the following exercises may be either nouns or verbs, but are used as one or the other in context.

1   Ask students to do the exercise individually, then check the answers with the class.

> **ANSWERS**
> 1 N   5 N
> 2 V   6 N
> 3 V   7 N
> 4 N   8 V

2   Ask students to do the exercise individually, then check the answers with the class.

> **ANSWERS**
> 1 Are you wearing a watch?
> 2 Many years ago there were no clocks.
> 3 Its shadow marked the movement of the sun.
> 4 They were able to determine midday.
> 5 After midday they had to move it 180 degrees.
> 6 At night it was impossible to tell time.
> 7 These clocks were popular in the Middle East.
> 8 Over the next few centuries the design was developed.

3   Ask students to complete the word web, then check the answers with the class.

> **ANSWERS**
> **Nouns:** blogs, post, information, stress, life, time, advice, breaks, idea
> **Verbs:** read, enjoyed, was, have, know, manage, was, want, thank

EXTENSION ACTIVITY

As a follow-up activity, you could ask students to write their own sentences using the words in the word web from exercise 3. You might also put the words on cards and give one set to each pair of students. Ask pairs to sort the cards into three piles: nouns / verbs / both. Then they could mix them up again and place them facedown in the middle of the table. Pairs take turns choosing a card, turning it over, and making a sentence using the word. Ask them to record them in their vocabulary notebooks.

WRITING Describing how to achieve a goal

Cultural awareness

Different languages have different ways of constructing sentences. Word order is quite fluid in some languages due to the use of inflections. English word order is quite rigid, and many students have trouble with this. Helping students to identify subject, verb, direct object [DO], and indirect object [IO] can help students write more clearly.

You may want to introduce your students to the idea of transitive and intransitive verbs at this point. In the *Macmillan Essential Dictionary*, these verbs are denoted as [T] and [I]. This distinction may help them understand when there is a DO and when there is an IO.

Before directing students to read the *Understanding sentence patterns* box, make sure they understand what a subject, pronoun, adjective, adverb, preposition, and prepositional phrase are. Ask students to read the *Understanding sentence patterns* box, and then check their comprehension. Ask: *In the first sentence, what is the subject? The verb? In the second sentence, what is the subject? The verb? The direct object?* Continue asking students to identify the parts of speech in the rest of the sentences.

1   Ask students to complete the exercise, and as a follow-up and for further reinforcement, you could ask them to underline the subject once, the verb twice, circle the direct object once, and circle the indirect object twice. Check answers with the class.

> **ANSWERS**
> 1 S + V   4 S + V + IO + DO
> 2 S + V + DO   5 S + V
> 3 S + V + DO   6 S + V + IO + DO

2 Ask students to complete exercise 2, then check the answers with the class.

> **ANSWERS**
> 1 Kevin plans to skip class. (S + V + DO)
> 2 Sachiko refuses to text. (S + V)
> 3 Lucas relies on his cell phone. (S + V + DO)
> 4 Omar has sent me five emails. (S + V + IO + DO)

Grammar

Background information

Gerunds look like verbs but function as nouns. In the following exercises, infinitives also function as nouns. This can be confusing to students who may view them as verbs. There is no hard and fast rule for which verbs can be followed by a gerund and which can be followed by an infinitive. Students may be uncomfortable with this lack of a clear rule. This would be a good time to introduce the idea that some words simply go together, or collocate, because historically that is the way they have been spoken.

1 Begin by introducing the idea of gerunds and infinitives on the board. Write *Jing enjoys ice cream.* Ask students to identify the nouns and other parts of speech. Then write *Jing enjoys running.* Ask them to identify the nouns and parts of speech again. Show them that in this sentence *running* looks like a verb, but it functions as a noun. Write some other examples, then move on to infinitives. Write *Shukang will plan the party. Shukang plans to study history.* Show how *to study* functions as a noun. Ask students if it is possible to say *Jing enjoys to run* or *Shukang plans studying history.* Then direct them to the *Grammar* box to find out the answer for themselves. Have a student answer the question, and then ask students why those sentences are not possible. Ask students to complete the sentences, then elicit the answers from the class.

> **ANSWERS**
> 1 to understand; working   4 writing
> 2 to miss; skipping   5 to keep / keeping
> 3 to speak   6 studying

2 Ask students to complete the conversation using the correct form of the verbs in the box. Check the answers with the class.

> **ANSWERS**
> 1 to take   4 to continue
> 2 to reduce   5 getting
> 3 to do   6 to think / thinking

EXTENSION ACTIVITY

On cards or slips of paper, write all the verbs from the *Grammar* box on page 24. Prepare a sheet with three columns labeled *Verbs followed by infinitives / Verbs followed by gerunds / Verbs followed by either.* Hand out the verb cards to pairs or groups of three students, and ask them to put them in the correct column. This could also be done as a competition to see which team can do it correctly in the quickest time.

WRITING TASK

This paragraph provides a model for students for the writing task. It is only a model, and students need to be made aware that there are many "right" ways of writing. The activities are designed to help students in their planning of their own paragraphs. Ask students to read the paragraph and follow the instructions. Then ask them to compare their answers with a partner.

> **ANSWERS**
> I like going for bike rides, and I love going for long walks. Unfortunately, I don't seem to have time for these things anymore. I'd like to have more free time for myself so I can do the things I enjoy doing. To achieve this, I will do several things. I plan to write down my appointments and then I will prioritize them. I hate to forget things, and this sometimes happens. I'll be more organized this way. I have a part-time job and I hope to reduce my hours from 15 to 12 hours per week. I also need to say "no" to my friends more. They often rely on me for homework help and I have to avoid saying "yes" every time. I want to be more honest and straightforward with them about my time commitments. If I achieve these things, I'll be able to have more free time.

Brainstorm, plan, and write

Encourage students to think about their own goals. As a class, you could brainstorm goals other than time management goals so that students can see a range of goals. Write the goals on the board for students to use in their writing. Then ask students to complete the chart with their own ideas.

When students have finished completing the chart, ask them to plan their paragraph and write a topic sentence. Allow them to refer to the model paragraph during the planning stage, but make sure they cover it up when they write their paragraph to avoid copying it. When students have finished planning, ask them to write a 100–150 word paragraph about their goals.

Cultural awareness

In some cultures, copying a text honors the author. You may want to discuss the idea of plagiarism in Western culture. Plagiarism is using someone's thoughts or ideas as your own.

Share, rewrite, and edit

Ask students to exchange their paragraphs with a partner. Encourage students to use the Peer review checklist on page 109 when they are evaluating their partner's paragraph.

Ask students to rewrite and edit their paragraphs. Encourage them to take into consideration their partner's feedback when rewriting.

Use the photocopiable unit assignment checklist on page 89 to assess the students' paragraphs.

Extra research task

There are many ways to calculate time. Ask students to find out what some of the different ways of keeping time are. Some examples are: Greenwich Mean Time (GMT), International Atomic Time (TAI), Coordinated Universal Time (UTC), Universal Time, Terrestrial Time, Barycentric Dynamical Time, and mean solar time. Encourage students to find other ways of keeping time. Another task would be for students to investigate which countries have daylight savings time and why daylight savings time has been implemented in these countries.

STUDY SKILLS Writing for the fearful

Background information

Writing can be a frightening or difficult thing for many students. They worry that they might make a mistake or they get frustrated because they can't find the word they want and looking up words in the dictionary takes a long time. This fear and frustration can lead students to writing less, when really, they should be writing more. Teaching students to write for fluency—without worrying about making mistakes— and trying to find a way to express themselves with whatever language they have will help build students' confidence and ability in writing.

The writing skills activities presented in this unit can be recycled again and again throughout the course and lend themselves well to a student journal (see *Study skills* section unit 6). Students can be encouraged to use different ideas each week as they write in a journal, or they can choose to use the same idea over and over if it works for them. Writing skills take time to develop, so encourage students to use the ideas to write often. It is also worth frequently spending 5–10 minutes of lesson time to try out the different ideas presented.

Start by asking students firstly what kinds of things they write and if they like to write (in English or in their own language). If not, find out why and write some of the reasons on the board. You may find that students say they don't like to write because they worry it is not correct or that they can't think of any ideas. Explain that writing in any language can be a difficult process, but that they are going to practice writing for fluency—trying to get ideas down without worrying about grammar or vocabulary, but only about expressing themselves. Promise them that you won't correct it! Turn their attention to the activities in the *Study skills* section for tips on generating ideas for writing.

Divide the class into four groups—A, B, C, and D. Ask all the As to read *Get the writing habit,* Bs to read *Write for five minutes,* Cs to read *Write from prompts,* and Ds to read *Make a life chart.* Once each group has had a chance to read and understand (and possibly discuss) their section, regroup the students so that there is an A, B, C, and D person in each group. Ask them to explain the section they read to the rest of the group. Elicit feedback from the whole class and discuss some of the things that they like / don't like about the exercises presented.

For this first free-writing session, either choose one of the exercises from the *Study skills* section to do with the entire class, or ask students to choose their own. You may find that some students struggle to write much this first time. Let them know that it is OK if they didn't get much on the page—in time, they will get better. Try to build in free writing practice into your lessons over the course. One way to really show students how much they have improved is to keep their first ever attempt and let them compare it to the last one they do at the end of the term. This could be a real motivator for students!

At the end of this lesson, use the video resource *Time flies as you get older*. It is located in the Video resources section of the Digibook. Alternatively, remind the students about the video resource so they can do this at home.

Reading	Highlighting Annotating
Vocabulary	Using explanations to find meaning
Writing	Brainstorming word maps
Grammar	*There is / are (+ quantifier) + noun*

Discussion point

Ask students to look at the picture on page 27 and say where they think it was taken. Initiate a discussion about the type of home in the picture. Ask: *Is it like your home?* You may want to introduce the following vocabulary: *apartment (flat—U.K.), house.* At this point, students may ask what the difference is between a house and a home. Ask them to save that question until later, as it comes up in the reading section.

Ask students to discuss the questions with a partner, using the sentence frames to help them get started. Photocopy and cut out the unit 3 *Useful language* page to provide some extra support. After pairs have discussed the three questions, have them share their answers with the class.

Vocabulary preview

Background information

Use the pictures on page 28 to introduce the paragraph about people in Mongolia. Find out if students know where Mongolia is and if they know what kind of homes the people live in. The top picture shows yurts, the types of tents that nomadic people in Mongolia live in. Ask students why they think they might live in big tents instead of houses. After completing the vocabulary exercise, you could ask students what they learned about nomadic people in Mongolia and find out if they have nomadic tribes in their country.

This section asks students to choose between two words, only one of which is correct in the context. This might be a good time to introduce some monolingual dictionaries into the classroom, but discourage students from using bilingual dictionaries to translate the words. By using a monolingual dictionary, students will see that there are different definitions for each word, and they will have to choose the best definition that fits the context.

Students can work individually or with a partner for this activity. If they work with a partner, ask one student to look up the first word in the sentence and the other student to look up the second word. Then ask them to compare definitions and choose the correct word. Ask them to add these words to their vocabulary notebook. You might point out which word pairs are opposites (antonyms) and provide synonyms for others. When the students have finished, do a quick whole-class check.

ANSWERS

1 location	5 resources
2 distinctive	6 lifestyle
3 typical	7 traditions
4 routine	8 unique

READING 1 Home is where the heart is
Word count 324

Background information

The terms *house* and *home* are not interchangeable. The word *home* has more of an emotional element for most people that is associated with a sense of security or belonging. It can refer to an actual dwelling where someone lives or finds refuge, or it can refer to a town or geographical area that someone feels connected to. Or, a home may not have any physical setting at all— it could be an emotional state one feels around people and communities, for example.

Because a "home" is so deeply connected with emotions, losing a home can profoundly affect someone. This is evidenced throughout human history. Native American and Aboriginal tribes suffered from forced relocation from ancestral homelands; communities relocated in dam building projects often lament the loss of their "home"; urban development projects which break up communities can cause feelings of loss.

For nomadic tribes, their way of life may be more linked to their concept of "home" than any physical setting, though, undoubtedly the regions in which they roam will have associations of "home." Traveling the same familiar routes would bring a sense of security and connectedness. (A Bedouin wouldn't feel "at home" roaming in North America, for example!) The fact that many nomadic tribes around the world are fighting to maintain their way of life shows the broadest sense of "home."

Before you read

The focus of this unit is on homes, so before you start, you may wish to get students interested in the theme by using the video resource *How our homes have changed*. It is located in the Video resources section of the Digibook. Alternatively, remind the students about the video resource so they can do this at home. Ask students what they think the difference is between a *house* and a *home*. Elicit a few answers, then refer them to the sayings. Ask them to discuss the sayings and say if there are any that they agree with more than others. Find out if students have any similar sayings in their own language. As a vocabulary building activity, you could ask students to brainstorm words that they associate with *home*.

Global reading

Remind students of the skill of skimming that they learned in unit 2. Ask them to tell you what skimming is and why it is important. Give students one minute to skim the article. Then ask them to do the exercise. You may want to give a time limit to deter students from reading too closely. The idea of skimming is to get the gist quickly. When students have finished, check the answers with the class.

> **ANSWERS**
> Paragraph 1: a (We don't find out much about Ibrahim, but we do find out about the typical routine of nomads.)
> Paragraph 2: b (Bedouin are just one example of nomadic tribes. The paragraph is about many different nomadic tribes.)
> Paragraph 3: a
> Paragraph 4: a (The main focus is on their homes—tents.)
> Paragraph 5: b

Close reading

1 Ask students to say where they found the information in the text that told them what the paragraph was about. Ask them to read the *Highlighting* box and then complete exercise 1. Some students may have highlighted different things. Discuss these differences and decide if they are main ideas or details.

Exam tip

Identifying *True*, *False*, and *Not Given* is an IELTS type task. It is important for students to understand that *False* means that the information in the text is the opposite of the statement given and that *Not Given* means that the information in the statement is not present in the text—that the text neither confirms nor denies the statement. Students may have trouble with *Not Given* because they often tend to bring their own interpretation to a text.

2 Ask students to do the exercise individually. When checking the answers, ask students to tell you where they found the answer in the text. There will be no information in the text for numbers 2 and 7.

> **ANSWERS**
>
> | | |
> |---|---|
> | 1 T | 5 T |
> | 2 NG | 6 F |
> | 3 F | 7 NG |
> | 4 T | 8 T |

3 Ask students to compare their answers to exercise 2 with a partner and discuss the questions. Draw students' attention to the words in the *Academic keywords* box and check their pronunciation. Ask students to add the words to their vocabulary notebooks.

Developing critical thinking

For question 1, ask small groups of students to write lists of the advantages and disadvantages of a nomadic lifestyle. Encourage them to use the words in the *Think about* box to help them with ideas. After the small group discussion, ask each group to report back to the class on what they thought were the advantages and disadvantages of a nomadic lifestyle. Then have them work in the same groups to discuss questions 2 and 3.

Extra research task

Ask students to research the different types of houses found in different countries. They could write a fact file: type of house, where it is, what it is made of, and why it is constructed the way it is (e.g. a highly pitched roof in a snowy country keeps the roof from collapsing from the weight of snow). Alternatively, ask them to research parts of the world where there are nomadic tribes. They could write a nomadic tribe fact file: name of tribe, where they are, clothing / body art, type of house, etc.

READING 2 Home automation

Word count 389

Background information

A gadget is similar to an appliance in that both are devices used for tasks; however, the word *gadget* has the additional meaning of being trivial or non-essential. Automation /ˌɔːtəˈmeɪʃ(ə)n/ has to do with using technology rather than humans to do tasks.

There are many gadgets in the modern home that are so ubiquitous that we soon forget that they are either fairly recent inventions or that many people did not have them in the recent past. It would be interesting to find out from students what items they find "essential." Is a TV essential? A phone? A washing machine? A refrigerator? A microwave? Air conditioning? None of these things were present in most houses 100 years ago, yet many people think of them as essential appliances today.

However, that is not to say that past generations did not have gadgets. Throughout history people have sought ways to save time and labor. Graters, colanders, toasting tongs, and rolling pins are among kitchen gadgets that no wealthy family could do without in the 1600s. The Victorian era saw an explosion in the number of household and nautical gadgets available. Many of these have been adapted to modern use—the hand-cranked ice cream maker, for example, now has an electric cousin. It would be interesting to know what items future generations will see as essential, and at what point seemingly quite non-essential gadgets cross over into the realm of "appliance."

Before you read

Introduce the topic of the next reading and make sure students understand the word *automation*. Ask them what they think home automation might be.

Make sure students understand what the pictures and items listed in the *Gadgets and appliances* box are, then ask students to discuss the questions with a partner. In feedback, ask students which objects they think are necessary appliances and which are not-so-necessary gadgets. (There may be differing opinions about this!)

Global reading

Give students two minutes to skim the text, then ask them to choose the best sub-title.

> **ANSWER**
> 2 The smartest home in the world

Close reading

1 Ask students to read the text and do the exercise, then check the answers with the class.

> **POSSIBLE ANSWERS**
> turns on lights
> waters the yard
> adjusts the thermostat
> opens the curtains
> answers the phone
> calls his children for dinner
> wakes him up
> opens his bedroom curtains
> starts his shower and sets the temperature
> turns on the TV news
> turns up the air conditioning
> monitors local weather
> informs him about traffic conditions
> keeps him updated on his favorite sports teams and scores
> monitors online activity
> suspends operation of their computers and TVs

Background information

Be sure to tell students that while it is OK to write in their own books, it is not OK to write in library books! This may seem obvious, but students don't always know the boundaries, and many university library books end up highlighted and annotated!

2 Annotating means *adding notes to*. Ask students if they ever write notes in the texts they read. Quickly brainstorm some things that students might write in a text, and ask students why they think it is a good idea to do this. After brainstorming, ask them to read the *Annotating* box. How many of their ideas did they find there?

After students have read the sample annotated paragraph, ask them to tell you what kinds of things it includes. Ask: *Why did the student write "Who is Ian Mercer?"? What does the word "change" refer to? What about "temperature controls"?* By drawing attention to the kinds of annotations made in the example, students will become more aware of the kinds of things they might like to write in their annotation of the text.

3 Ask students to compare their annotated texts and discuss the questions. Check pronunciation of the words in the *Academic keywords* box and ask students to add them to their vocabulary notebook. You may want to review these words in a later lesson.

Developing critical thinking

1 Ask students to discuss the questions in groups. For question 1, refer them to the words in the *Characteristics* box. When they have finished, ask them to share their ideas with the whole class.

2 Remind students of the text *Home is where the heart is*. Ask them if they think there is a connection between this text and *Home automation*. Then ask them to discuss the questions in groups. Encourage them to use the words in the *Think about* box to give them ideas. When the students have finished, ask them to share their ideas with the class.

Vocabulary skill

Using explanations to find meaning will help students develop their reading skills and help curb their reliance on translators. Remind students about the vocabulary skill they learned in unit 1 (using examples to find meaning). Ask them if they can think of other ways to find the meaning of new words without looking them up or using a translator. Then ask them to read the *Using explanations to find meaning* box. You could ask students to annotate the example by circling the word *consult* and the explanation *asking for specialist advice*, and then drawing a line connecting the two. They can then use the same annotation technique when they complete the next two activities.

1 Ask students to write the definitions of the words in bold, then check the answers with the class.

> **POSSIBLE ANSWERS**
> 1 make changes
> 2 do something when you are far away from it
> 3 shuts down

2 Ask students to write the definitions of the words in bold, then check the answers with the class.

> **POSSIBLE ANSWERS**
> 1 area
> 2 work with
> 3 develop

WRITING Describing your home

Writing skill

> **Background information**
> By now students will be familiar with word maps because they have done brainstorming activities on the board. Word maps are very useful tools. Because of their graphical, non-linear nature, they allow freer planning that encourages connecting concepts. Word maps may be unique to each individual because different people will make different connections. For more information about word maps (also known as spidergrams, mind maps, spidergraphs), search online to find a video of mind map creator, Tony Buzan. His company also has free mind map software you can download to create your own.

1 Begin by asking students to read the *Brainstorming word maps* box. Then ask them to name some of the advantages of brainstorming in this way. They may resist at first, but keep encouraging them to answer. Then ask them to create a word map for a paragraph describing their family.

2 Ask students to compare their word maps with a partner and discuss the differences.

Grammar

There is / There are can be quite a difficult grammatical concept for students to understand because the subject actually comes after the verb. Check that students are comfortable with the construction *There is / There are* and the terms *count / noncount nouns* before beginning the grammar section. On the board, write: *A book is on the table.* Ask students to give you another sentence that means the same thing. Prompt them to produce: *There is a book on the table.* Do the same with a plural sentence, e.g. *Some apples are on the table → There are some apples on the table.* Ask students why in the first sentence we use the singular form of the verb, *is*, and in the second, we use the plural form, *are*.

Once students understand the idea that the thing being referred to (*book / apples*) determines which verb form to use, ask them to tell you which to use with this sentence: *There _____ water in the glass.* Point out that *water* is a noncount noun, so it requires *is*. Ask them to read the information in the *Grammar* box.

Afterwards, check that they understand which quantifiers go before a count noun and a noncount noun. You could play a game. Ask students to close their books. Write COUNT NOUNS on one side of the board and NONCOUNT NOUNS on the other side. Call out the quantifiers and ask students to tell you which category they belong to.

1 Ask students to complete the sentences individually, then do a quick whole-class check.

ANSWERS

1	is	5	is
2	are	6	are
3	are	7	is
4	is	8	are

2 Ask students to circle the correct quantifier, then check the answers with the class.

ANSWERS

1	one	5	a
2	much	6	some
3	few	7	a
4	great deal of	8	many

For some free practice, ask students to look at the picture on page 34 and write three to five sentences about what they see, e.g. *There are lots of houses. There are only a few cars. There is one swimming pool.*

3 Ask students to do the exercise individually, then share their answers with a partner.

WRITING TASK

This paragraph provides a good transition from the grammar section to the writing task. Ideally, it should be done on a different day from the grammar section in order to provide some review. Tell students they are going to read about someone's home. Ask them to follow the instructions. After reading, check the answers, then initiate a short discussion by asking students if the apartment is similar to their home or not.

ANSWERS

I live in an apartment building. It's about 30 minutes from the city center. There are a lot of similar apartment buildings around mine. There are a few small stores near us but there aren't any nice restaurants or cafes. My building is 18 stories high and I live on the seventh floor. There are five main rooms in the apartment. When you enter, there is a large living room. The kitchen is next to it. There are two bedrooms—one for my parents and one for my little sister and me. I like the apartment a lot, although it is small. There is only one bathroom and there are not many closets. Someday I'd like to have a bigger home with more closets.

Brainstorm, plan, and write

Encourage students to think of as many ideas as they can about their home. Invite them to add more circles to the word map if they like. Circulate and ask questions that will prompt more ideas. Ask students to look back at the unit and find more words that they can add to their word map. Once they have finished, ask them to explain their word map to another student. This may prompt some more ideas that they can then add.

Ask students to look at their word maps and decide which area they will discuss in their writing first, second, third, etc. Point out that the circles provide natural subtopics for organizing the paragraph.

To help with writing topic sentences, ask students to think of a sentence that will introduce the paragraph. To illustrate this, write a few sentences on the board: *My kitchen is next to my bedroom. I live near a park. My house doesn't have many closets. I live in a small but beautiful house.* Any of these sentences could be topic sentences, but none of them would be the topic sentence for the same paragraph. With the students, identify the main idea in each sentence. This will give an idea of what the paragraph will be about. You could ask: *Which sentence introduces a paragraph about not having much room to store my stuff? Which introduces a paragraph about where I live? Which introduces a paragraph about my kitchen? Which introduces a paragraph about my home?* Hopefully, students will see that the topic sentence needs to contain the key idea of the paragraph.

When the students have finished planning, ask them to write a 100–150 word paragraph about their home.

Share, rewrite and edit

Ask students to exchange their paragraphs with a partner. Encourage students to use the Peer review checklist on page 109 when they are evaluating their partner's paragraph.

Ask students to rewrite and edit their paragraphs. Encourage them to take into consideration their partner's feedback when rewriting.

Use the photocopiable unit assignment checklist on page 90 to assess the students' paragraphs.

STUDY SKILLS Reviewing and practicing vocabulary

Getting started

Begin by asking students how they review vocabulary at home. Brainstorm some ideas, then ask them to do the experiment. When the students have finished, elicit some feedback on the experiment.

> **Background information**
> The words in Group 2 are easier to remember because they are grouped into categories: the top row is about the classroom or school, the second is a list of colors, the third is about feelings, and the fourth contains words that describe the dimensions of an object.

Ask students why they think Group 2 is easier to remember, and ask them how they can apply this categorization concept to their own learning and recording of vocabulary. Remind them that word maps provide another way of categorizing vocabulary.

Scenario

If students have been keeping vocabulary notebooks, then this will be a great opportunity to review the way they are recording their vocabulary. Typically, students will simply write the word and the translation next to it. Although this method may work well at lower levels with concrete vocabulary, it has many limitations at the higher levels when students are learning more abstract words. Some good practices students could use for recording vocabulary include writing the part of speech, how the word is pronounced, how it can be used, an example sentence to show its use in context, clues about which words might go with it, thematic organization of the words so they can be easily accessed when writing, etc.

Ask students to do this exercise with a partner. Elicit whole-class feedback from one pair and check to see if the rest of the class agrees.

> **POSSIBLE ANSWER**
> Lucy works hard and uses definitions, examples, and pictures. However, she should review the words more and try categorizing them.

Consider it

As a class, generate a list of good practices students could use for recording their vocabulary. Ask them to copy the list and keep it in a place where they can refer to it often. After students have discussed the tips with a partner, check the answers and ask the class why each tip is a good idea.

> **ANSWERS**
> *Students' own answers*

Over to you

Ask students to discuss the questions with a partner. Monitor the activity and elicit feedback. Ask students to make a list of the best ways to record vocabulary so that they can study it better. Give each pair a turn to share their list with the class, and write their ideas on the board. Ask the class to copy the full list and keep it in a place where they can refer to it often.

UNIT 4 SIZE

Reading	Predicting
	Making inferences
Vocabulary	Using definitions to find meaning
Writing	Writing compound sentences
Grammar	The present progressive tense

Discussion point

Ask students to refer to the picture on page 37 as they discuss the questions. For question 1, you could brainstorm big and small animals. Photocopy and cut out the unit 4 *Useful language* page to provide some extra support. After students have discussed the three questions, have them share their answers with the class.

Cultural awareness

Both sayings in question 3 are common sayings in English. You could exploit this question further by giving students some more small / big idioms and asking them to figure out the meanings, e.g. *He's a big fish in a small pond* (= He's important in a small organization, but wouldn't be important in a larger one); *Don't sweat the small stuff* (= Don't worry about small things); *He's small fry* (= not important—small fish); *She's the big cheese* (= the boss); *The Big Apple* (= New York City); *I have bigger fish to fry* (= I have more important things to do); *The bigger they are, the harder they fall* (= the more powerful someone is, the harder it is for them to accept when they lose power). Then ask students if they have any similar idioms in their language.

Vocabulary preview

1 Because the words in exercise 1 are new and out of context, students could use their monolingual dictionaries to look up the words. Since the definitions in the dictionary will be slightly different from the definitions given here, students will have to employ deeper thinking processes to complete the exercise. Encourage students to look beyond the first definition for the definition that most fits the examples. The answers have been divided up in order to make the task easier—the first five words are linked with a–e and the next set with f–i. Students may also wish to write down the part of speech—this will help them complete exercise 2. Be sure to review the pronunciation of the words and encourage students to add them to their vocabulary notebook.

ANSWERS

1 e	4 b	7 h
2 d	5 c	8 i
3 a	6 g	9 f

2 Ask students to complete the sentences using the words from exercise 1, then check the answers with the class.

ANSWERS

1 abundant	4 massive	7 approximately
2 demand	5 Aside from	8 efficient
3 population	6 primary	9 concentration

READING 1 Fuel of the sea

Word count 446

Background information

Krill is a traditional food in many countries, for example Japan and Korea. Whales are also still hunted by some communities. Proponents of whale hunting explain that it is a cultural tradition. Inuit tribes in North America, for example, are allowed to hunt a certain number of polar bears and whales a year in order to feed their communities. Information and beliefs about the healthy properties of fish and krill have led to a market demand for these in other parts of the world which is, in turn, putting pressure on the populations in the ocean. You may need to be sensitive to cultural differences of opinion on this matter.

Before you read

1 This could be done as a class discussion, with pairs, or in groups. Tell students not to worry if they don't know the answers, as they will find them in the article.

Exam tip

Although predicting cannot be tested in an exam, it is, nonetheless, an important exam skill. Students may have trouble with this if they are not knowledgeable about a diverse range of subjects, so it is a good idea to encourage students to read a variety of informational texts. Students may also think that predicting is unimportant in a time-pressure exam situation. Impress on them the importance of predicting as a timesaving strategy and one that will enable them to read more effectively. It is important to note that predicting doesn't just happen before reading starts; it also happens during reading. Good readers use textual clues to predict the next sentence or next paragraph.

Remind students about the strategy of previewing from unit 1. Ask: *Why is it important to preview?* Check students' understanding of *predict / prediction*, then ask them what kinds of information they can predict about a text from the pictures, titles, and headings. Refer them to the *Predicting* box. Check their understanding of predicting. Ask: *While you are reading, when do you make predictions? What do you do if your predictions are wrong? Why is predicting important?*

2 Using the pictures on pages 38 and 39 and the title of the article, ask students to predict what the title means.

Global reading

Give students two minutes to quickly skim the article to see if their prediction was correct.

> **ANSWER**
> 2 Krill are a primary food source for many sea animals.

Close reading

1 Before asking students to read, remind them of the questions they discussed in the *Before you read* section. Ask them to read the text to check the answers to those questions.

> **ANSWERS**
> Blue whales eat krill.
> Blues whales eat about four tons of food each day.
> Some penguin populations are decreasing in number because there are fewer krill, their food source.

2 Ask students to write answers to the questions. Direct them to the words in the *Academic keywords* box to give them ideas. Discourage them from using dictionaries or translators, but invite them to look up words for homework.

> **ANSWERS**
> 1 Krill are tiny, shrimp-like animals.
> 2 They live in all the world's oceans.
> 3 Whales, fish, seals, and penguins eat krill.
> 4 Krill swarms can get as large as 450 square kilometers.
> 5 Loss of sea ice, demand for krill oil, and fishing are causing krill numbers to decline.
> 6 Some animals that feed on krill, such as penguins, have declined in number.

Developing critical thinking

SUPPORTING CRITICAL THINKING

For this discussion, students need to develop an argument based on what they have read. Encourage students to use the information in the text as the basis for their opinions. For example, students might say that scientists should make people more aware of the importance of krill in the ecosystem so that people stop using krill oil in dietary supplements. Using information to formulate ideas and opinions is an important academic skill.

Ask students to work in groups to discuss the questions. To support the discussion, ask students to make a chart. On one side they list the reasons krill numbers are declining, and on the other side they list things marine biologists or people could do to reverse the decline. When the students have finished their discussions, have them share their ideas with the class.

EXTENSION ACTIVITY

Ask students to design an informational poster that would raise awareness of this issue within the wider school community. Alternatively, students could be asked to write a speech for the school to persuade students to help reverse the decline in krill populations.

Extra research task

Ask students to find out what companies such as Whole Foods Market® and organizations such as Greenpeace are doing to study and help krill. Another task might be to research overfishing and sustainability.

READING 2 Size doesn't matter
Word count 419

Background information

Singapore is multiracial, multicultural, and multilingual. Its four official languages—English, Malay, Mandarin, and Tamil—reflect the main nationalities that live there, and most Singaporeans are at least bilingual. Students are taught in English because Singapore was once a British colony, but they are also taught their own mother tongue as a way to preserve their cultural heritage. Singapore is multireligious as well, with many Malays following Islam.

Before you read

1 Ask students to look at the picture on page 40 and answer the questions.

2 Have students answer the questions using the characteristics in the *Think about* box. Ask two or three students to share their responses with the rest of the class. Check students' pronunciation of the phrases in the box, *Singapore*, and *Asia*.

3 Check that students understand the meaning of *doesn't matter* (= it's not important). Then ask them to look at the picture and title of the article on page 41, and predict what it will be about.

Global reading

Ask students to skim the article and check their predictions.

Close reading

1 Ask the students to read the article and complete the sentences. When they have finished, ask them to compare answers. Then ask one student to read the sentences aloud with the correct answers so that you can check how well students are able to say numbers. You may need to provide a quick numbers review exercise.

Background information

Inferring information from a text is a difficult but important skill for students. It is difficult because it requires interpretation of information that is not explicitly stated in the text. Like a detective, students have to look for clues in the text. Students may think they don't know how to make inferences, but you can show them how they do it every day.

2 Introduce the idea of making inferences by giving the students some scenarios such as the one in the *Making inferences* box. For example, someone is holding their foot with a pained expression on their face. What can you infer? Or your mother walks into your room and says, "This room is a mess!" What can you infer? You will have to make your scenarios culturally relevant, of course.

After students have read the *Making inferences* box, check their understanding by asking them to think of an everyday example of when they infer.

Draw students' attention to the words in the *Academic keywords* box and check their pronunciation. Ask students to add them to their vocabulary notebooks.

Developing critical thinking

1 Ask students to discuss the questions in groups. Refer them to the ideas in the *Think about* box. When they have finished, ask them to share their ideas with the whole class. Encourage them to give reasons and justifications for their views.

2 Remind students of the text *Fuel of the sea*. Ask them if they think there is a connection between this text and *Size doesn't matter*. Remind students to use the language in the *Think about* boxes to help them formulate their ideas. Then ask them to discuss the questions in groups. When the students have finished, ask them to share their ideas with the class.

Extra research task

Students may wish to research the multicultural aspect of Singapore. They could find out more about the different cultures, languages, or foods of Singapore. If they are interested in music or art, they could research some popular singers or artists.

Vocabulary skill

Ask students if they can remember what vocabulary skills they learned in Units 1 and 3. If necessary, ask them to look back at the units. Write the two skills under the heading *Vocabulary skills* on the board (*Using examples to find meaning*, *Using explanations to find meaning*). Tell students that they are now going to learn how to find the meaning of new words by looking for definitions. Make sure they understand the term *definition*, and ask them to read the *Using definitions to find meaning* box. Afterwards, ask them to close their books and tell you some of the words and punctuation that signal definitions.

1 Ask students to do the exercise but discourage them from using a dictionary as this would undermine the purpose of the exercise. When they have finished, check the answers with the class.

2 Ask students to use the definitions in the box to complete the information about Singapore, again without using their dictionaries. Then check the answers with the class.

ANSWERS
1 a small country at the tip of the Malay Peninsula
2 an island resort at the southern end of the country
3 Indian, Chinese, and Malay influences
4 a large, smelly, and spiky fruit
5 one of the Asian "tigers"

3 Ask students to complete the definitions, then check the answers with the class. After completing all three exercises, ask students to write some of the new vocabulary in their vocabulary notebooks. Then check their pronunciation.

POSSIBLE ANSWERS
1 large
2 about or not exactly
3 plentiful
4 *Demand*
5 *population*

WRITING Describing how your neighborhood is changing

Writing skill

In order for students to understand the concept of compound sentences, they need to understand what an independent clause is. Write a simple sentence on the board, e.g. *Whales eat krill*. Ask students what the subject is and what the verb is. Underline the subject once and the verb twice. Now write *Krill eat plankton*, and underline the subject and verb again. Point out that these are independent clauses because they are complete thoughts: they can stand alone and they have a subject and a verb. Point out that they are very short and simple. Ask students how they could combine the sentences into one longer sentence, for example: *Whales eat krill, and krill eat plankton*. Again, underline the subjects and verbs. Point out that there are now two subjects and two verbs—two independent clauses—and the sentence is called a compound sentence.

Ask students to give you more examples of words that can combine two independent clauses to make a compound sentence. Ask them to read the *Writing compound sentences* box and find more examples. After reading, check that the students have understood the difference in use between *and, but, or,* and *so*. Point out the use of commas. Ask students why there are no commas in the sentence: *Whales and penguins eat krill*. (*Whales and penguins* is the subject, and this is a simple sentence, not a compound one.)

Cultural awareness

Students from some cultures have a hard time with punctuation because it either doesn't exist in their language, or it is used differently. Students may not understand what all the fuss is over such a small mark! You may like to show how the comma is a short pause, and the period at the end of the sentence is a longer pause. Read some sentences and emphasize the pauses. Unit 5 looks at punctuation in more detail.

1 Have students circle the correct conjunctions in bold. Then ask them to underline the subjects and verbs in the sentences. When going over the answers, ask different students to read parts of the passage aloud to practice pronunciation and exploit the text further. Make sure they pause at the commas and periods, and use a falling intonation.

ANSWERS
1	and	6	so
2	so	7	but
3	or	8	or
4	so	9	but
5	and	10	so

2 Have students combine the sentences. Check that they have included the comma in the combined sentences where needed. Ask them to underline the subjects and verbs.

ANSWERS
1 The signs in Singapore are in English, so it is easy to get around.
2 There is a park in my neighborhood, but no one goes there.
3 You can easily get a taxi on the street, or it is easy to call for a taxi.
4 I have a lot of friends in my neighborhood, and they all live nearby.

Grammar

In this section, students will learn to use the present progressive to talk about actions happening now. To introduce the topic, look around the room and describe what is happening. Once you have modeled two or three sentences, ask students to give you some more examples of what is happening in the room (or out the window or in the hallway). You could also use a picture to elicit responses.

Ask students what tense they are using to describe what is happening now. Ask them to read the *Grammar* box to find out another way that the present progressive tense can be used. Check their understanding. You may also need to remind students of some spelling rules:

- for verbs ending in *-e*, drop the *e* and add *-ing*: *take* ➜ *taking*.

- for verbs that follow the C+V+C (consonant, vowel, consonant) pattern and have either one syllable or two syllables where the stress falls on the second syllable, double the final consonant: *hop* ➜ *hopping*; *begin* ➜ *beginning*.

- for verbs that end in *-ie*, change the *ie* to *y* and add *-ing*: *lie* ➜ *lying*.

Certain verbs are not usually used in the present progressive (also called present continuous), though in popular music and culture you may hear examples to the contrary. (Take, for example, the famous slogan "I'm lovin' it!" from McDonald's®.) Verbs of state are normally used in the present simple because they are not actions, but states of being. You may want to make this distinction with your students before doing exercise 2. Examples of verbs not usually used in the progressive tense are: *love, like, hate, want, think, believe, hear, need, remember, understand, know, agree,* etc.

1 Ask students to complete the paragraph using the present progressive form of the verbs in the box, then check the answers with the class.

> **ANSWERS**
>
> | | |
> |---|---|
> | 1 is changing | 5 am paying |
> | 2 are buying | 6 is making |
> | 3 are investing | 7 are starting |
> | 4 is pushing | 8 are shopping |

2 Ask students to work individually to do the exercise, then check the answers with the class. Use the context in exercises 1 and 2 to point out some of the time phrases used with the present progressive tense—*right now, these days*. Encourage students to brainstorm more time phrases. Explain that these phrases need only be used once to set the context.

> **ANSWERS**
>
> | | |
> |---|---|
> | 1 a are closing | b know |
> | 2 a are beginning | b wants |
> | 3 a is taking | b needs |
> | 4 a are planning | b Are you saving |

For some extra practice using the present progressive tense, ask students to make guesses about the picture on page 44, e.g. *I think they are building … They aren't working now because …*

WRITING TASK

Ask students to read the model paragraph and work individually to do the exercise. When they have finished, check the answers with the class.

> **ANSWERS**
>
> My neighborhood is changing a lot. Some of these are positive changes, but some are negative. More people are moving into the neighborhood. This is a positive thing. These new residents are shopping in the neighborhood, so they are spending money locally. This helps local businesses a lot, and develops a sense of community. A lot of new buildings are going up as well, but I don't think this is a good thing. It is creating a lot of noise, and many of the new homes are sitting empty. There are now a lot of new homes, but there are some older, empty homes. There are more children in the neighborhood now, but no one is building more parks, and I know we will need more of these in the future. Overall, I think the way the neighborhood is changing is a positive thing.

Brainstorm, plan, and write

In this section, students brainstorm and write their ideas in a table. Because the task expects students to talk only about positive and negative changes and their effect, the table is a good way to focus the brainstorm. Ask students to compare their ideas with other students if they are having trouble thinking of ideas. Feel free to allow them to make up information!

Remind students of the importance of a broad topic sentence. Ask them to identify the topic sentence in the writing task model.

When students have finished planning, ask them to write a 100–150 word paragraph about their neighborhood. If you have been assigning the writing task to students to do for homework, it would be a good idea to have them do some writing in class. There are several reasons for this. First, you can observe the writing process that individual students use. Do they make a plan? Do they use a dictionary or translator? Do they become distracted easily? You may be able to make suggestions to help students become more efficient as writers. Second, practicing writing under time pressure can help prepare students for time constraints in tests and exams. Third, you can be sure that the student is producing his/her own work and not getting help at home. Finally, you will get a full class set of writing turned in which you might not get if students forget to do their writing homework!

Share, rewrite, and edit

Ask students to exchange their paragraphs with a partner. Encourage students to use the Peer review checklist on page 109 when they are evaluating their partner's paragraph.

Ask students to rewrite and edit their paragraphs. Encourage them to take into consideration their partner's feedback when rewriting.

Use the photocopiable unit assignment checklist on page 91 to assess the students' paragraphs.

checklist on page 109

Extra research task

You could ask students to interview their parents, grandparents, or someone in their community about the changes they see happening in their neighborhood or community. You could also ask students to research a particular area of technology that is changing rapidly: cell phone technology or computer technology, for example. They could then write a paragraph or do a poster presentation about the changes and the effects they are having.

STUDY SKILLS Process writing

Background information

For many students, writing is not a process. They think that if they mimic a model answer, then their writing will be good. While there are certainly good arguments for using a model to help structure a piece of writing, students also need to be aware that their first effort needs to be revisited in order to make it better. As there is no "right answer" in writing, there are many different ways to discuss a topic. Sometimes students need to rethink how they have written something in order to make it clearer, better organized, or more accurate.

The stages of writing that students have been introduced to in *Skillful* are designed to help students think about this process. In this writing structure, students first come up with ideas without thinking about grammar. This ideas phase is important for enriching the content of the paragraphs. Students then create a plan, which is a crucial step in creating a well-organized piece of writing. After writing, students share their work in order to find out if their ideas make sense to other people. Finally, they edit to correct any errors in clarity, structure, and grammar. Only then do they submit it to the teacher. This process also encourages learner autonomy that will help students become independent learners.

It may be necessary to emphasize to students that as their level of English progresses, process writing will become more and more important, especially as their writing tasks become longer. This *Study skills* section opens up a discussion about the process that students have been using in the last four units so that students can become more aware of its importance.

Getting started

You might want to open up the discussion by asking students to think about how they write in their own language and how they write in English. Ask them to discuss the questions with their partners, keeping the way they write in mind. Afterwards, open the discussion up to the class. You may want to put some of the students' ideas on the board to refer back to after completing the *Study skills* section.

Scenario

Ask students to do this exercise with a partner. Elicit whole-class feedback from one pair and check to see if the rest of the class agrees.

POSSIBLE ANSWER

Chen wrote his assignment in a quiet study space and had his friend give him feedback. He also revised his paper afterwards. However, he should have edited his paper carefully for spelling, punctuation, and grammar errors before he handed it in.

Consider it

After students have discussed the steps with a partner, check the answers and ask the class why each step is important.

ANSWERS

Chen did these steps: pre-writing, writing, sharing, revising, submission.

Over to you

You may want to revisit the discussion from the beginning and emphasize that these steps are important when students are writing in their native language as well as when they are writing in English.

You may also want to show students how to use the spell checker, if they do not know. Emphasize that it is a useful tool, but it is not perfect! It may suggest spellings that end up being a different word than the one intended. Spelling (and grammar) checkers are useful, but should only be used in addition to the students' own editing. At the end of this lesson, you could use the video resource *Reaching for the skies*. It is located in the Video resources section of the Digibook. Alternatively, remind the students about the video resource so they can do this at home.

UNIT 5 PATTERNS

Reading	Determining main ideas and supporting details Taking notes
Vocabulary	Adding prefixes for negation
Writing	Using end punctuation and capitalization
Grammar	Giving advice and making suggestions

Discussion point

The focus of this unit is on animals, so before you start you may wish to get students interested in the theme by using the video resource *Spots and stripes*. It is located in the Video resources section of the Digibook. Alternatively, remind the students about the video resource so they can do this at home.

Ask students to discuss the questions with a partner, using the sentence frames to help them get started. The picture on page 47 shows fields bisected by a road and question 1 refers to it. For question 2, students should look around the room. Photocopy and cut out the unit 5 *Useful language* page to provide some extra support. Students may have some difficulty with the expression *patterns of behavior*. Ask them to think about what it might mean. You could give examples, such as *I can't go to sleep at night, and I am always tired in the morning*. After students have discussed the three questions, have them share their answers with the class.

EXTENSION ACTIVITY

A way to extend the vocabulary of patterns is to ask students to bring in swatches of cloth or cutouts from magazines showing different patterns. They could make a poster by gluing the patterns onto cardboard and labeling them. You could hang them up around the classroom and have the students walk around and discuss the different patterns, e.g. *I like this striped pattern because … This pattern is interesting because …*

Vocabulary preview

Students may need a dictionary to do this exercise, but discourage them from using translators or bilingual dictionaries. Be sure to practice pronunciation of the words and ask students to record them in their vocabulary notebooks. When they have finished, check the answers with the class.

ANSWERS
1 b   2 c   3 a   4 d   5 g   6 e   7 f

READING 1 Time for a change
Word count 481

Before you read

Refer students to the picture of the man running on page 48. Ask them to think about why he might be running and how it relates to a bad habit. Ask: *Is he exercising? How is he dressed? Where do you think he is going?* etc.

ANSWER
The picture shows a man running because he is late.

For the discussion, refer students to the sentence frames and the *Bad habits* box under the picture. You could also conduct this activity as a *Find someone who …* drill. Ask students to make a 2×5 grid on paper. Down the left column, ask them to write five bad habits (they can use the ones in the box or think of their own). Ask them how to make a question to find out if someone has a bad habit, and write it on the board for reference, e.g. *Do you … (bite your nails)?* Then ask students to move around the classroom asking other students if they have the habit. When they find someone with the bad habit, they write that person's name in the right-hand column. In order for students to talk to as many people as possible, you could make a rule that they can only write each person's name down once. As a follow-up, find out who has which bad habit.

Background information

Life coaching is a concept that may be unfamiliar to students. Life coaches help people figure out their own personal goals and how to achieve them. It is a form of counseling in the way that mentoring is, but it is not psychology or psychiatry. It is a growing field, and more and more people are training to become life coaches or seeking inspiration and assistance from them.

It may be interesting to find out from students if life coaching exists in their culture or to discuss why they think life coaching is popular in the U.S. and U.K. In the student's culture, who would they seek to get advice from? It may be that for students from cultures in which the extended family plays a greater role, life coaching is done by family members for free.

Global reading

It's important to keep reminding students of the reading skills learned in previous units. Ask students to tell you what they should always do before reading (look at the pictures, title, sub-title) and what this is called (previewing). Ask them to preview the article on page 49 for 15 seconds, close their book, and then tell you what they think it is about and where they think it comes from. Then ask students to predict what they will read. Ask them to read the four options, then give them three minutes to skim the text. After three minutes, ask them to stop and check the correct topic.

> **ANSWER**
> 2 Ideas for breaking bad habits.

Close reading

Exam tip

Picking out the main ideas in a text is an important critical thinking skill and one that students will encounter in exams. Many students have difficulty determining which is the *main idea* and which is the *supporting detail*. This can affect their reading as well as their writing. In English writing, the main idea is usually located in the topic sentence, which is generally the first sentence of the paragraph. This is not always the case, however, so students should not just choose the first sentence. Another clue is that main ideas tend to be broader in scope. Details will be examples or evidence to support the main idea.

Introduce the topic by asking students to tell you what they think the term *main idea* means (the most important, the key). Then ask them what they think *supporting details* means (something that tells more about the main idea). Finally, ask them to read the *Determining main ideas and supporting details* box. Check their comprehension before asking them to do exercise 1.

1 Preview the *Academic keywords* box with students before asking them to read *Time for a change*. Check students' pronunciation of the keywords and ask them to record them in their vocabulary notebooks. When the students have finished, check the answers with the class.

> **ANSWERS**
> 1 a M   b S
> 2 a M   b S
> 3 a M   b S
> 4 a M   b S
> 5 a M   b S

2 After students finish exercise 1, ask them to say what helped them decide whether the sentences expressed the main idea or a supporting detail. Verbalizing how they made that decision will help them formulate the strategy in their mind and will help those students who didn't get them right see the kinds of clues they need to be looking for.

As a follow-up to the discussion, you could ask students which advice they found the most useful. Then ask students to do exercise 2 individually. When they have finished, check the answers with the class.

> **ANSWERS**
> 1 d   2 e   3 a   4 c   5 b

Developing critical thinking

Read aloud the words in the *Bad study habits* box and explain them as needed, e.g. *cramming* (= studying hard in order to learn a lot in a short time). Encourage students to discuss their answers to the questions in a group and give reasons for them, using the sentence frames and the words in the box for help and ideas. You may find that some students do all the talking during discussions and some do not do much talking. To ensure that everyone in the group participates in the discussion, give each person three to five "speaking chips." These can be tokens or simply slips of paper. When a student answers one of the questions, they can put their chip in the middle of the table. They must get rid of all their chips by the end of the discussion, and once they have used all their chips, they can't speak again except to ask someone their opinion!

READING 2 The Fibonacci sequence
Word count 565

Background information

The article gives information about the Fibonacci sequence in nature and architecture, but the sequence is also present elsewhere. Music by Mozart is supposed to contain the sequence, and it has been argued that Roman poets structured their poetry using it. There are many examples of the sequence in art—often referred to as the golden ratio. Fibonacci numbers (and the golden ratio) are used in furniture design and even in finance. A power station in Turku, Finland has neon Fibonacci numbers down one of its chimneys.

Before you read

The pictures on page 50 recall the discussion at the beginning of the unit on patterns. Students may be familiar with the concept of fractals from mathematics in which the same pattern repeats itself. Ask students to discuss the question with a partner, then share their ideas with the class.

Global reading

Ask the students to preview and skim the article and check the best sub-title. Check the answers with the class.

Close reading

1   Remind students of the note-taking skills they learned in unit 3 (highlighting and annotating). Ask them to highlight key information in the article and also to annotate it.

In this unit, students will learn to take notes based on a text. This is a key skill when doing research or when reading a text with information that they want to recall later. Good note taking involves writing down key information clearly and in an organized way. Poor notes are of no use, so stress to students the importance of taking good notes.

Start by finding out what students do when they take notes. Brainstorm some ideas on the board, and then ask them to read the *Taking notes* box. See how many of the ideas in the box are similar to their own. Take each of the points in turn and discuss them further:

Title and date—Why do you think this is important, especially when taking notes for class?

Highlighted and annotated text—How will these help?

Cards, notebook, paper—Do you have a special notebook or system for keeping track of notes? Why is it important to have an organized system?

Use symbols, abbreviations, etc.—What symbols and abbreviations do you use? (You may want to give students some ideas about common symbols, e.g. i.e., w/, @, RE, etc.) How can color help?

Copying word for word—Why is it important to put things into your own words? (Emphasize that the process of putting things into your own words aids comprehension and retention of concepts. It is an important step in the learning process. Also, it means you can avoid plagiarism.)

Reviewing—Why is this step important?

2   Ask students to look at the notes and say what techniques have been used. Afterwards, ask them to take notes on the rest of the text and compare them with a partner. Stress that there is no right way to take notes, and we can all get ideas for new techniques from each other. You may want to ask early finishers to write their notes on an overhead transparency to be shared with the class later.

3   Draw students' attention to the words in the *Academic keywords* box and check their pronunciation. Then ask them to read the sentences, decide if they are true or false, and correct the false sentences. When students have finished, check the answers with the class.

Developing critical thinking

You may have noticed that some groups are able to carry on their discussion for longer periods of time than others. Some lower level students may need help with some of the language of discussions. Before putting students into groups for the discussions, brainstorm a couple of ways to ask for an opinion (*What do you think? Do you agree?*), give an opinion (*I think … In my opinion …*), agree politely (*Yes, I agree with you. Yes, I think so, too*), and disagree politely (*No, I don't think so. I don't really agree*). Make sure everyone feels comfortable using the phrases, then ask students to try to use at least three in their discussion.

1   Ask students to discuss the questions in groups, then share their ideas with the whole class.

2   Remind students of the text *Time for a change*. Ask them if they think there is a connection between this text and *The Fibonacci sequence*. Then ask them to discuss the questions in groups. Draw their attention to the *Patterns in nature* box. When the students have finished, ask them to share their ideas with the class.

Vocabulary skill

Brainstorm the opposites of some of the terms that have come up in this unit to introduce the idea of prefixes for negation. Remind students of some of the terms they have encountered—*lazy, positive, efficient*—and ask for their opposites. They may say *not lazy, not positive* or *negative, not efficient*. Ask if there is another way to say *not efficient* and try to elicit *inefficient*. Refer students to the *Adding prefixes for negation* box.

Background information

Although it is not possible to predict these prefixes with 100% accuracy, there are some broad guidelines:

ir- only comes before words beginning with *r*

im- only comes before words beginning with *p* or *m*

il- only comes before words beginning with *l*

Students will need to learn the prefixes for each word and will need to consult a dictionary to check them. They may wish to dedicate a certain part of their vocabulary notebook to recording common examples of words and their opposites.

1 If you have access to a projector connected to a computer, you can show the students the *Macmillan Dictionary* online (http://www.macmillandictionary.com/) before they complete exercise 1. Although the dictionary does not list antonyms, it is possible to check that you have used the correct prefix by typing in the word. So, for example, if you type in *irrealistic*, you get a message saying, *"Sorry, no search result for irrealistic. Did you mean …"* and a list of words. If you look down the list, you can find *unrealistic*. This way of searching for the right answer even when the answer is wrong is a helpful strategy for students and can help them become more independent. The online dictionary also has pronunciation. If you click on options, you can choose either American or British pronunciation. This is a great way for students to check and practice their pronunciation at home.

ANSWERS

1 unrealistic	7 irresponsible
2 dissatisfied	8 inconsiderate
3 unpopular	9 impersonal
4 irrational	10 unbelievable
5 inefficient	11 illegal
6 impolite	12 disrespectful

2 Ask students to do exercise 2 individually. When they have finished, check answers with the class.

ANSWERS

1 I am disorganized.	6 Your answer is incorrect.
2 It is impossible.	7 It is illogical.
3 It is illegal.	8 It is unlikely.
4 It is irregular.	
5 It is unrealistic.	

See how many opposites students can remember at the beginning of the next lesson. Say the word and ask students to call out the opposite. Or, do it as a quick team competition.

WRITING Giving advice in an email

Cultural awareness

Unit 4 explained that students from many cultures have difficulties with punctuation, often because they do not have the same rules in their own language. Students from cultures that use a writing system other than the Roman alphabet have a lot of problems with capitalization, so it is worth spending some time discussing the rules for capitalization. Similarly, students may not recognize that a space comes *after* the punctuation, not before.

To introduce the topic, write some letters randomly on the board, some capitalized and some not. Ask students what the difference is between the letters and introduce the word family *capital / capitalization / to capitalize*. Then elicit ideas about when they should capitalize letters. Next, write the symbols . /, / ? on the board and ask students to name them. Refer students to the *Using end punctuation and capitalization* box, and ask them to check their answers and to find the rules for capitalization.

1 Ask students to do exercise 1 individually. When reading out or checking answers, remind students that periods signify a long pause and falling intonation, a comma is a shorter pause and falling intonation, and a question mark uses rising intonation for a *yes / no* question and a falling intonation for information questions.

When conducting feedback on this activity, use the projectable Digibook, if possible, so that students can annotate and correct on top of the exercise.

POSSIBLE ANSWERS

1 a Guess what! I solved this math problem—finally! I hope it's correct.

 b Congratulations! I know math is not your favorite subject.

2 a Did you hear about Maggie? She cut up all her credit cards!

 b She did? I knew she wanted to change some of her shopping habits.

3 a Quick! Look over there!

 b That's amazing! But what, exactly, is it?

2 Ask students to do the exercise individually, then check the answers with the class.

ANSWERS

1 The Fibonacci numbers can be seen in the Taj Mahal in India.

2 Please ask Mother and Father what time dinner is.

3 Today is Tuesday, April 13.

4 Is the test on Monday or Tuesday?

5 My favorite book is *Of Mice and Men*.

6 Venezuela is a country in the northern part of South America.

7 Omar speaks English, Arabic, and French.

8 Drive west until you get to the town of East Dayton.

9 Mr. and Mrs. Peterson moved to New York City last summer.

10 The Red Sea separates East Africa from the Arabian Peninsula.

Grammar

Background information

Students may not notice that *should* does not change in the third person singular, but *need to* and *have to* do.

In the affirmative, the modal *should* and the verbs *have to* and *need to* can all be used to give advice, with *need to* and *have to* being used for stronger advice. However, only *should* can be used in the negative for giving advice. *Don't need to* and *don't have to* are used for lack of necessity and are not dealt with in this section. By focusing on the function (giving advice), students should be able to use these forms easily. Creative students may try to use the negative of *have to* and *need to*, but should be informed that they have a different function and that for this exercise, only the affirmative should be used.

Another point you may want to mention to students is that the pronunciation of *have to* and *need to* is shortened to /hæftə/ and /ni:dtə/ when speaking. This is especially important in listening. In informal writing, students can use the contracted form *shouldn't*, but in formal academic writing, contractions should not be used.

The other grammatical structure introduced here (*It is* + adjective + *to* + base form of the verb) may cause some confusion because it does not really have meaning. Focus on the overall meaning, and teach the structure as a chunk rather than trying to break it down.

Introduce the section by presenting a scenario and asking students for advice (e.g. *My friend is really having trouble getting to sleep at night. I want to help him. What should he do?*). Elicit some ideas and write them on the board without the modals, e.g. *drink milk before bed, read a book, listen to soft music.* Once you have a few ideas, you can orally reiterate: *So you think he should drink milk before bed? That's a good idea. And he needs to go to bed earlier? Yes, he could try that. You think it's helpful to read a book? These are really good suggestions.*

1 Ask students to read the *Grammar* box, and then ask concept check questions to make sure they have understood what they read. Make sure they are aware that *need* and *have* change form and that *should* does not. Help students practice pronunciation. Ask them to do exercise 1 and when they have finished, check the answers with the class.

ANSWERS

1 It is good to make shopping lists.

2 You should buy things on sale.

3 You should not eat out so much.

4 It is important to take public transportation.

5 You have to open a savings account.

6 You need to keep a budget.

7 You should be careful with your credit cards.

8 It is not good to buy designer goods.

2 Ask students to do the exercise, then check the answers with the class.

ANSWERS

1 You ~~needs~~ to address the person first.

2 You should ~~to~~ include a clear subject line.

3 It is ~~a~~ good to keep things short and simple.

4 It is important **to** remember that emails are permanent.

5 It is ideal to ~~should~~ answer email right away.

6 You should not ~~wrote~~ **write** things you would not say.

7 You should ~~checking~~ the email before you send it.

8 It**'s** not good to type in capital letters.

WRITING TASK

Although, arguably, emails between friends needn't follow conventions of spelling and capitalization, they do need to have some consistency. This email has lots of mistakes, and it provides a good opportunity for students to practice their editing skills. After they have underlined the modals and expressions used to give advice, ask them to correct the text. Ask them to compare answers to see if someone else found something they missed.

ANSWERS

To: Terry@email.com

Subject: my advice

Hi **T**erry,

I got your email last **S**aturday asking me for my advice about studying in **L**ondon. First, congratulations**!** I'm happy you got accepted. My **s**ummer program there was great. Are you also planning to start the program in **J**uly**?**

There are some excellent professors there**.** You <u>should</u> write to **P**rofessor Radison. She can help answer some questions, too. I will send you her email. They have a booklet for new students called "Tips for **N**ew Students" and I'm sure she will send you that**.**

<u>It's good to</u> arrive early so you can get settled before classes start. <u>It's important to</u> reserve an early place if you want to live in the dorms**.** <u>You need to</u> apply for a place before **M**arch. You <u>shouldn't</u> worry, though. I think there is plenty of time**.** Or are you going to rent an apartment**?** I'm really glad I can help. Write me back with specific questions**.**

Robin

Brainstorm, plan, and write

As a warm-up for this activity, brainstorm some student problems and write them on the board, e.g. *what to get your girlfriend for her birthday; whether to play football with your friends or go to dinner with your parents;* etc. Next, ask students to tell their partner about their (not too serious) problem and ask them for some advice. Then pairs swap roles and repeat.

Tell students they are going to write to a friend to give them some advice on one of the topics in the box. Ask them to choose a topic and complete the table.

As an alternative, ask students to first write an email asking for advice on one of the topics in the box. Then have them "send" it to another student, who must answer the email by giving advice. This could be done more authentically using email if you prefer.

Students will need to think about how to begin their email. They may wish to refer to the email model, but ask them to use it as a guide only—not to copy it. They will also need to plan how to organize the advice. Once they have a plan, ask them to share it with a partner. Then they should choose at least four of the best ideas to include.

When students have finished planning, ask them to write a 100–150 word paragraph. Students could do this electronically if you wish. Ask students to send their email giving advice to you or to their partner. If emailing is not feasible, you could copy and paste the email template onto a handout and the students could write their emails on that.

Share, rewrite, and edit

Ask students to exchange their email with a partner. Encourage students to use the Peer review checklist on page 109 when they are evaluating their partner's email.

Ask students to rewrite and edit their emails. Encourage them to take into consideration their partner's feedback when rewriting.

Use the photocopiable unit assignment checklist on page 92 to assess the students' emails.

STUDY SKILLS Where does the time go?

Background information

Time management is one of the skills that many students lack and is an important developmental step towards better autonomy and independence. Many students won't have considered how they spend their time, so teachers can help raise their awareness through some time management training. This *Study skills* section helps to raise students' awareness of how they spend their time and helps students set their own time management goals.

Set this activity up a few days before doing it in class. Ask students to keep a record of what they do each hour for a few days and bring it to class on the day you do the *Study skills* section. Encourage them to be honest, as they will not be turning anything in.

For the time circles, you can either ask students to draw their own or you can create some on the computer to hand out in class. It is important that the circles are numbered to represent the 24 hours in a day. You could draw an example on the board.

The first circle should be how students use time *now*. Encourage them to use different symbols or colors to represent the different activities. Ask them to reflect on how they use their time, referring to the questions in the *Study skills* section.

The second circle should be how students *want* to use their time—possibly during the school year rather than during the holidays since part of the aim of the activity is for students to set goals which will help them be better students. Ask them to be realistic and healthy in their goals; they can't aim to sleep for only three hours a night in order to fit everything else in, for example! Some students might like to draw a weekly circle and a weekend circle to represent how they would like to spend their time differently.

When they have finished, they may like to share and discuss their images, though don't insist on it. Ask them to reflect on the changes that they need to make in order to achieve their new time-use goal.

UNIT 6 SPEED

Reading	Distinguishing facts from opinions Identifying tone
Vocabulary	Organizing new words: adjectives and adverbs
Writing	Using commas and colons
Grammar	Comparative forms of adjectives and adverbs

Discussion point

Background information

The picture on page 57 shows a horse race, but there may be other types of races (greyhound, Formula 1, camel, marathons, etc.) depending on the culture of the students. You could start the discussion by asking: *What types of racing do you have in your country? Is it popular?* Avoid discussions about betting on the races where gambling is illegal, especially Islamic countries.

Before you start, you may wish to get students interested in the theme by using the video resource *A need for speed*. It is located in the Video resources section of the Digibook. Alternatively, remind the students about the video resource so they can do this at home.

Ask students to discuss the questions with a partner, using the sentence frames to help them get started. For questions 2 and 3, you may need to prompt lateral thinking—ask students to think about mealtime customs, driving, vacations, etc. Photocopy and cut out the unit 6 *Useful language* page to provide some extra support. In a mixed culture class, you may find that different cultures do things differently. If you are in a monoculture class, you could compare students' answers with your own culture. After students have discussed the three questions, have them share their answers with the class.

Vocabulary preview

Students will need to use their monolingual dictionaries for this activity. Before beginning the exercise, ask students what part of speech they think fits in the blank space. Point out clues such as *a* or *an* or *the*, which signal that a noun is needed. Also point out that an adjective can come between the article and the noun (as in number 3: *a steady ...*). You could also ask students to underline the subject and verb in the sentence as was done in unit 2. This will help students see if a verb is needed in the blank. Be sure to check students' pronunciation of the words and ask them to add the words to their vocabulary notebooks.

ANSWERS

1 appeal	5 origin
2 impact	6 emphasized
3 pace	7 advocate
4 associate	8 functional

READING 1 Hurry up and slow down!

Word count 554

Background information

The slow movement and others like it are becoming increasingly popular as life gets more hectic and stressful. The International Institute of Not Doing Much (IINDM) website has articles which aim to teach people how to slow down and do less. They even sell a button which reads, "Multitasking is a moral weakness."

Taking time to enjoy life rather than rushing through it is not a new concept, though. W.H. Davies published a now well-known poem in 1911 entitled *Leisure*. The last two lines of the poem could serve to reinforce ideas espoused by slow movement advocates:

A poor life this is, if full of care,
We have no time to stand and stare.

Before you read

1   Use the picture on page 58 to introduce the topic. Ask: *What is he holding? When do you use a stopwatch?* Ask pairs to use the words in the *Actions* box to discuss the question.

EXTENSION ACTIVITY

If your class is an active one, you could follow it up by staging a little competition. With pairs or as a class, ask: *Who can say the alphabet the fastest? Who can remember five words from the previous lesson the fastest? Who can name three small animals?* etc. Most students will have stopwatch capabilities on their cell phones, so they can time each other if you choose to do the activity with pairs or in groups.

2   Test students by asking them what they should do before reading—elicit *preview* and *predict*. Ask them to preview the title, headings, and pictures in the text for one minute, and then tell you what they think it is going to be about. Ask: *What do you think the title means? How does the picture relate to the title? What kind of article is it?* (an interview).

Global reading

Ask students to check their predictions from *Before you read* exercise 2.

Close reading

SUPPORTING CRITICAL THINKING

Students are introduced to two skills in this section: identifying purpose and distinguishing facts from opinions. Identifying the writer's purpose is important because it enables the reader to make judgments about the content and about how carefully to read. If the purpose is to inform, for example, then the reader may need to read the information more carefully. If the purpose is to persuade, then the reader may need to think about who the writer is and what his/her hidden agenda might be. Identifying purpose involves inferencing skills—the purpose may not be overt, but textual clues will inform the reader.

Distinguishing facts from opinions can be tricky for students who may take everything at face value without questioning whether it is fact or opinion.

Both skills are tested in language exams, so students planning to take an exam will need to develop these skills.

1 To introduce the topic, ask students why people write articles. Elicit some responses and write them on the board. Then ask students to read the article and complete exercise 1.

ANSWER
1 inform

Afterwards, ask them why they think the article's purpose is to inform. What led them to that decision? (e.g. *It gives facts and information about the Slow Movement; it's written in a light but serious tone—not funny; it's not trying to convince them to buy anything or join anything.*) Compare it to *A Matter of Time* in unit 2 which uses a lot of imperatives.

2 After students have read the article, ask them if it gives facts or opinions. Then ask students to read the *Distinguishing facts from opinions* box. Check students' comprehension by giving some examples (*Water turns to ice below zero degrees Celsius; Paris is a lovely city,* etc.), then ask them to complete exercise 2.

ANSWERS
1 O   2 O   3 F   4 O   5 O

Be sure to check pronunciation of the words in the *Academic keywords* box and ask students to put them into their vocabulary notebooks.

Developing critical thinking

Before the students discuss the questions, ask questions to find out their reaction to the article. Ask: *What do you think about the Slow Movement? Is there a Slow Movement in your country?* Divide students into groups to discuss the questions. Draw their attention to the ideas in the *Reasons for slowing down* box. You may want to put together students who do not normally work together so that they have more opportunities to speak to a wider range of people. Encourage students to invite less talkative students to talk more. After students have discussed the questions, ask them to share their ideas with the whole class.

READING 2 Keeping up with the Tarahumara
Word count 463

Before you read

You may need to introduce the expression *ways of getting around* before the students discuss the questions. Ask them to look at the *Ways of getting around* box and ask: *What are all the words related to?* (transportation) *What do you think "ways of getting around" means?* (modes of transportation). Draw attention to the pronunciation of the phrase *get around* /gedəraʊnd/, and make sure students connect the final consonant sound with the initial vowel sound. Ask pairs to discuss the questions using the sentence frames and transportation words to help. After students have finished, do a class poll to find out how the students get around.

Global reading

Background information

The title of the article, *Keeping up with the Tarahumara,* is a take off on the expression "keeping up with the Joneses." This expression means *trying to match the lifestyle of your neighbors* (who may be wealthier) or *trying to have the material possessions that they have.* So, for example, if they buy a new car, you buy a new car. If they put in a swimming pool, you put in a swimming pool. *To keep up with* has another, more literal meaning—to stay at the same pace as someone else, for example, *My son runs so fast that it is hard to keep up with him.* So, the title has a double, somewhat humorous meaning.

The expression *to keep up* is quite commonly used, so it is worth teaching. (*Keep up! You're walking too slowly! I can't keep up with all my assignments,* etc.) Your students may be interested in the double cultural meaning, but if they are likely to get confused, then only teach them the second, more literal meaning of the expression.

Ask students to read the title of the article and guess how the expression *keeping up with* relates to the picture. Ask them to look at the map and identify which part of the world it depicts. Ask them to predict what the article is going to be about. Finally, ask them to quickly skim the article for two minutes and answer the global reading question.

ANSWER
2 The tradition of long-distance running among the Tarahumara

Close reading

SUPPORTING CRITICAL THINKING

Identifying purpose and tone, and distinguishing facts from opinions are both important critical thinking skills that are introduced and practiced in this unit. Using these skills helps the reader learn more about the author's intent and, in turn, gives the reader heightened insight into the text. As students move further along in their academic reading, they will need to be able to recognize tone so that they can evaluate material more carefully.

Remind students of one of the skills they learned with the last reading—understanding purpose. Ask them what they think the purpose of this article is. Ask them if they think the article is serious or funny, and introduce the word *tone*. Write *tone* on the board in the middle of a word map with the words *serious* and *funny* coming off the center circle.

Brainstorm some other tones that a piece of writing might take. Ask students to read the *Identifying tone* box and find other examples. Point out that *humorous* = *funny* and the opposite is *dry*; the other word pairs are also opposites.

1 Ask students to read the text and decide what the author's tone is. Deter students from using dictionaries. When students have finished, ask them to highlight the clues that helped them make their decision.

ANSWERS
2 admiring

2 Ask students to check their answer to exercise 1 with a partner and discuss the question. Then check ideas with the whole class.

POSSIBLE ANSWERS
runs effortlessly, remarkably, such good runners, incredibly, famous in the running world, admired as world-class athletes

3 Ask students to write complete sentences for their answers. This is a good opportunity for writing practice. When students have finished, check the answers with the class.

ANSWERS
1 They live in the canyon country of northern Mexico.
2 It means "foot runner."
3 A pueblo is bigger than a rancho.
4 They grow corn and beans.
5 Their running courses may be anywhere between 48 and 160 kilometers long.
6 Victoriano got first place.

4 Remind students what they learned about inferring meaning in unit 4. Ask them to use these skills to look for clues that will help them infer meaning.

ANSWERS
Statements you can infer: 1, 2, 4, 5, 6

Point out the words in the *Academic keywords* box from the text and ask students to add them to their vocabulary notebooks.

Developing critical thinking

1 Find out if there are any runners in the class. If there are enough runners, you could divide the groups up so there is at least one runner in each group. Encourage students to give reasons for their opinions and to contribute to the discussion. Refer them to the ideas in the *Think about* box for question 2.

2 Remind students of the text *Hurry up and slow down!* Ask them if they think there is a connection between this text and *Keeping up with the Tarahumara*. Then ask them to discuss the questions in groups, using the ideas in the *Characteristics* box to help them. When the students have finished, ask them to share their ideas with the class.

Extra research task

The article depicts a traditional way of life for the Tarahumara that has been noted by people in other parts of the world and is being studied and copied. Students who are interested in sports and running could explore the influence the Tarahumara running method is having on runners elsewhere (search for *Tarahumara method of running* or *toe strike method*). Other students might like to investigate running shoes since more and more people are advocating running in more traditional ways—barefoot or in thin-soled shoes and sandals. Alternatively, students may wish to investigate other people who are known for running or for some other feats of endurance.

Vocabulary skill

As a lead-in to the *Vocabulary skill* section, ask students: *How do I feel?* Then mime some emotions (happy, sad, etc.). Next, ask students: *How am I doing this?* Mime some actions (e.g. driving a car) in a certain way (e.g. happily). If students say *drive a car happy*, say, *Yes, I am driving a car happily.* Do this a few more times until the students get the idea of doing something − −*ly* (slowly, quickly, etc.). On the board write some adjectives and adverbs:

adjective	adverb
happy	happily
quick	quickly

Show students that an adjective describes a noun, but an adverb describes an action (or verb), e.g. *My mother is happy. She drives happily.*

You could also ask students to stand and mime some adverbs. Give a student the adverb and ask him/her to do an action in the manner of that adverb (as you have done). Ask the other students to guess the adverb. If students need more help thinking of actions, you could give them an action and the adverb to mime. They could also do this with partners.

Tell students that adverbs do not always end in -*ly*, so they need to understand more about adjectives and adverbs. Ask them to read the *Organizing new words: adjectives and adverbs* box.

1 After students have read the examples in the box, ask them to circle the nouns that the adjectives refer to (e.g. *local* ➔ *traditions*; *dietary* ➔ *habits*) and draw a line to the verb that the adverb refers to (e.g. *live* ➔ *slowly*; *join* ➔ *soon*, etc.) Then ask students to complete exercise 1. When they have finished, check the answers with the class.

> **ANSWERS**
> 1 ADV   5 ADV
> 2 ADJ   6 ADJ
> 3 ADV   7 ADJ
> 4 ADJ   8 ADJ

Using the sentences in exercise 1, ask students to circle the nouns that the adjectives refer to and draw a line to the verbs that the adverbs refer to. Then ask students to say which question each adverb answers (1 how?; 3 how often?; 5 when?).

2 Ask students to complete the sentences individually. When checking the answers, ask them if they have used an adjective or an adverb.

> **ANSWERS**
> 1 sometimes   5 comfortable
> 2 now   6 there
> 3 careful   7 famous
> 4 slow   8 quickly

WRITING Making a comparison

Writing skill

> **Background information**
> As with the punctuation and capitalization in unit 5, students from certain countries will have problems with commas and colons because they do not occur in their language. In some languages, commas are used quite differently—in place of periods, for example, so an essay can be one long sentence!

1 To lead in to this section, ask students to name the foods in the picture on page 63. Write them on the board in the sentence: *I can see tomatoes carrots peppers chilies …*, leaving out the commas. When you have finished, ask students if they can see anything wrong with the sentence on the board. If they need prompting, read the sentence quickly without pausing or dropping your intonation between the foods. Hopefully, this will prompt the students to say that there are no commas. With students who tend to overuse commas, write two or three sentences on the board: *Running is good, because, it is healthy; I run, every day.* Review the rules for commas, periods, and capitalization. Then ask students to learn more about commas and colons by reading the *Using commas and colons* box. Afterwards, check their comprehension and ask them to complete exercise 1. After students have completed the exercise, ask them to identify which rule each sentence uses.

> **ANSWERS**
> 1 You will need to bring three things: a notebook, pens, and a calculator.
> 2 A lot of people like to travel at high speeds, but I hate it.
> 3 Like many people, I have an online profile.
> 4 She works all day. In addition, she takes classes at night.
> 5 If I can give you one piece of advice it is this: exercise.
> 6 Before you start running, it is good to do a 15-minutes warm-up.
> 7 I love to run, but my friends hate to run.
> 8 My father always says, "Slow down! No one is going to take your food away."

2 This activity provides students with practice for editing their own work. Ask students to try it on their own, then ask them to compare answers with a partner before checking answers as a class.

writing

ANSWERS

Since its formation, the Slow Food Movement has been an international organization that promotes food culture as an alternative to fast food. It has these aims: encourage farming, preserve food traditions, and protect cultivation techniques. It was established as part of the Slow Movement. However, it has since grown as a movement in its own right. There are offices in eight countries: Italy, Germany, Switzerland, the U.S.A., France, Japan, Chile, and the U.K. Carlo Petrini, its founder, is still active in the movement. To spread the message to a younger generation, volunteers teach gardening skills to students.

Grammar

Before introducing this section, you may need to review the concept of syllables. Ask students if they know what a syllable is. Say the word *syllable*, clapping on each syllable. Ask: *How many syl-la-bles?* as you clap on each one. Give some more examples with words from the unit (e.g. *lo-cal, slow-ly, soon, quick-est*, etc.).

To introduce the idea of comparative forms, find or bring in pairs of objects that are the same (e.g. two students' book bags, a couple of balls, pens, etc.). Show students the objects and say: *This is big, but this one is bigger. This is new, but this one is newer*. Ask a student to compare two objects. Tell students they are going to read about comparing things using adjectives and adverbs, and then ask them to read the *Grammar* box. As there is a lot of information in the box, ask questions to check students' comprehension, e.g. *When do we add –er? How many syllables in are there in* old? *How many are there in* older? *Why aren't there two es in* safer? *Why are there two gs in* bigger? *What happened to the –y in* happier? *Why do we say* more modern *and not* moderner? *What is different about* good, bad, *and* far?

Be sure to draw students' attention to the bottom of the box, which shows how the comparative forms are used in sentences with *than*.

1 Ask the students to complete exercise 1, and check their pronunciation of the comparative forms.

ANSWERS

1 easier	7 more easily
2 more famous	8 worse
3 bigger	9 better
4 better	10 slower
5 wider	11 faster
6 more noisily	12 farther / further

As a follow-up, ask pairs to compare some of their personal items (cell phones, watches, books, etc.).

2 Ask students to complete the exercise. Then check the answers with the class.

ANSWERS

1 Lions can run faster than horses.
2 Joe ran the race more quickly than Tom.
3 Oscar travels farther / further to school than Noor.
4 Beth's grade on the exam was worse than Alex's.
5 Chicago is hotter than New York.
6 Tim can run for longer than Kenzo.
7 Chemistry 103 is more difficult than Chemistry 101.
8 An airplane ticket is more expensive than a bus ride.

WRITING TASK

The first task requires students to recall all the information from the *Writing skill* section, so it is useful as a review. It also helps students with their editing skills. To lead in to the section, ask students to look at the picture and say what it shows. Then ask them to read the paragraph and do the task. When the students have finished, check the answers with the class.

ANSWERS

I shop in both supermarkets and convenience stores. Both have their plusses and minuses, but overall I prefer to shop in convenience stores. Supermarkets are bigger than convenience stores. Therefore, they take longer to get through. I feel they are also more impersonal. There is a lot of choice in a supermarket, but I don't need all that choice. The food is fresher in supermarkets than in convenience stores. However, the lines are always longer. I can get through the lines more quickly in a convenience store. Convenience stores often stay open later, so are, of course, more convenient. The prices in convenience stores are almost always higher than in supermarkets, but I usually try to buy things on sale. In fact, there are three things I never buy in convenience stores: fruit, vegetables, and meat. If I want them, the supermarket is better.

After students have completed the exercise, ask them to tell you what they think a convenience store is and how it differs from a supermarket. Ask students if they shop in convenience stores, supermarkets, or markets.

Brainstorm, plan, and write

You may need to model this activity on the board before asking students to complete their own chart. Draw a chart on the board that is identical to the one in the book. In column 1, write *cat* and in column 2, write *lion*. Down the left-hand column, write *size, speed, character, ability*. Ask students to compare a cat and a lion, and write the words in the relevant columns (see example).

	1 cat	2 lion
size	smaller	bigger
speed	slower	faster
character	friendlier	more aggressive
ability	climbs well	doesn't climb as well

Ask students to choose one of the four topics in the box and complete the table for that topic.

Ask students to share their ideas with a partner and talk through a plan of their paragraph. Ask them to try to include adjectives and adverbs. Ask them to think carefully about the topic sentence they will use.

When students have finished planning, ask them to write a 100–150 word paragraph. This could be done in class or for homework. For those students who always write short paragraphs, encourage them to try to reach 115 or 120 words this time.

Share, rewrite, and edit

Ask students to exchange their paragraphs with a partner. Encourage students to use the Peer review checklist on page 109 when they are evaluating their partner's paragraph.

Ask students to rewrite and edit their paragraphs. Encourage them to take into consideration their partner's feedback when rewriting.

Ask students to turn in both their first and second drafts so that you can see how much editing and improvement they have made. Choose a paragraph that has big improvements from the first to the second draft. Type each up verbatim without revealing the student's name. Show the class the first draft and the second (either on the projector or as a handout), and ask them what improvements were made. Use the photocopiable unit assignment checklist on page 93 to assess the students' paragraphs.

STUDY SKILLS Keeping a journal

Getting started

Background information

Students may be confused about the difference between a diary, a personal journal, and a professional journal. A personal journal is a place to reflect on experiences and thoughts. A diary is a place to record things that happened during the day, but not necessarily to reflect on them. A professional journal is a published body of work on a specific topic. Many books and movies have been written as diaries and journals, for example, *Robinson Crusoe, The Diary of Anne Frank, Bridget Jones's Diary.* Keeping a written journal in the language you are learning is a great

way to practice writing. Blogs are modern versions of journals published online. Although to an older generation it may seem odd that younger people want to publish their thoughts for anyone to read, the line between private and personal space is now becoming blurred.

Some students like to keep an oral journal—to record themselves instead of writing. This is a great way to practice speaking skills and could be suggested for those students who are resistant to the idea of writing.

Lead in to the topic by finding out if any students keep a record of what they do every day, or if they write about their thoughts and feelings in a notebook or on a blog. If so, find out what kinds of things they record and why they write one. How private is their journal? Who reads their blog? Introduce the expression *to keep a journal* to ensure they know what it means. Then ask students to discuss the questions with a partner.

Scenario

Ask students to do this exercise with a partner. Elicit whole-class feedback from one pair and check to see if the rest of the class agrees.

POSSIBLE ANSWER
Fatima writes every day and she writes in a place where she feels comfortable. However, she should write more quickly and not worry so much about her grammar, spelling, and punctuation.

Consider it

Ask students to read the five tips for starting a journal and add any others that they think might be useful. After students have discussed the tips with a partner, ask the class why each tip is a good idea. For example, ask: *Why is it important to be calm? Why should you not worry about spelling, grammar, and punctuation?*

Over to you

Ask students to discuss the questions with a different partner. Monitor the activity and elicit feedback.

EXTENSION ACTIVITY

You could ask students to begin writing a journal in English to record their thoughts and experiences of their learning. There could also be a place in which students ask you questions related to the course.
Collect the journals periodically to check them, but avoid correcting mistakes—they should be places where students can reflect freely without worrying about making mistakes.

If you want to revisit writing for comparison, ask students to write a paragraph comparing oral and written journals, or writing blogs and traditional journals.

UNIT 7 VISION

Reading	Scanning
	Using a chart to organize your notes
Vocabulary	Adding suffixes to change verbs into nouns
Writing	Writing complete sentences
Grammar	Count and noncount nouns

Discussion point

Cultural awareness

Perceptions of color vary according to culture. Some cultures may view two colors as the same while another culture perceives them as different. For example, people who have spent their entire life in a certain environment do not distinguish between green and blue, but identify different greens as different colors, which to our eyes look the same. So, color perception can vary according to the environment a person lives in.

A second cultural distinction is what different colors mean. In Western culture, green is the color of envy and also luck. White symbolizes purity, which is why brides tend to wear white. Red is the color of anger or passion, and black symbolizes death or evil. It would be interesting to find out what associations different colors have for your students. They could research this issue further after they do the writing task.

Before you start, you may wish to get students interested in the theme by using the video resource *Learning to see*. It is located in the Video resources section of the Digibook. Alternatively, remind the students about the video resource so they can do this at home.

Ask students to look at the picture on page 67 and guess what it is. Why do they think there are so many colors? Ask them to discuss the questions with a partner. Photocopy and cut out the unit 7 *Useful language* page to provide some extra support. After students have discussed the three questions, have them share their answers with the class.

EXTENSION ACTIVITY

After students have discussed question 3, you could extend the activity in a couple of ways:

1) Ask students to tell you why they think color is used in idioms, e.g. ask: *Why a white lie? Why not a green lie?* (*white* = innocence, purity. It is an innocent lie.) Discuss what the different colors mean. Students could make a chart comparing what colors symbolize in Western culture and in their culture.

2) Find out if students have any color idioms in their cultures. Ask them to translate them and explain what they mean.

ANSWERS

to tell a white lie = to tell a small, unimportant lie
to see things in black and white = to see things as all good or all bad
to see red = to be extremely angry
to do something once in a blue moon = to do something rarely (N.B. A blue moon occurs every two to three years. Seasons have three full moons to make 12 full moons a year. Every two to three years, there is an extra lunar cycle. So, a blue moon is an extra full moon that occurs to make four full moons in that season.)
to be in a gray area = to be in an area that is not clearly defined (e.g. not black and not white)
to give someone the green light = to give permission to do something (refers to the traffic signal)

Vocabulary preview

Students will need to use their monolingual dictionaries for this exercise, though they may be able to figure out some words by looking at internal clues. *Background*, for example, has the word *back* in it, so its meaning may be inferred. *Horizontal* may be inferred from the word *horizon*. Point out these clues to students to help them build strategies for deciphering new vocabulary. When they have finished, ask them to identify the part of speech of each word and to underline the stressed syllable. Ensure that they are able to pronounce the words and ask them to add them to their vocabulary notebooks.

ANSWERS

1 b	2 a	3 a	4 a	5 a	6 b	7 b	8 b

READING 1 Is seeing really believing?

Word count 395

Before you read

Background information

It takes most people longer to do the second experiment (saying the colors) than the first (reading the words). This is because of interference. When looking at a word, we see both its color and meaning. If the two are different, we have to make a choice. Because experience has taught us that word meaning is more important than the color a word is written in, interference occurs when we try to pay attention only to the color. This classic psychology experiment is called the Stroop Effect.

To lead in, ask students if they have ever done brain-training exercises. Tell them they are going to warm up their brains before they read today. In question 1, students read the words, ignoring the color. In question 2, they say the color, but ignore the word. Ask pairs to time each other. When pairs have finished, ask them to share their results with the class.

Global reading

1 Ask students to preview the article and tell you the type of article it is (possibly a blog site) and where it probably came from (the Internet). Then ask them to skim the article for 90 seconds and answer the question.

> **ANSWER**
> 2 Optical illusions

Exam tip

Scanning is an important exam skill because it saves time. If students know that they just need to look for the answer to a specific question, they can just scan the text to find that answer. Many students make the mistake of thinking that they have to understand the entire text when often they just need to understand enough to find the answers to the questions. As a result, many do not finish the exam because they have spent too long on one part. Scanning is something that we do in everyday life and in academic work. When we look up the meaning of a word or check the details of something reported in a newspaper, we are scanning for information.

2 Begin by asking students to recall all of the reading skills they have learned so far in Units 1–6 (skimming, fact versus opinion, main ideas versus supporting ideas, predicting, making inferences, previewing). Write the skills on the board, and tell students that they are going to learn another important skill: scanning. Ask students what they know about scanning. Explain that scanning is what they do when they go onto a website and look for specific information, for example. Ask them to read the information in the *Scanning* box. After reading, ask students why it is not necessary to start at the beginning of the text and how it is possible to predict where the information might be (e.g. using headings as clues). Tell them they are going to scan the article for color words. Ask: *Without reading, where can you predict you will find some of the color words?* (in the paragraphs with lines pointing to the pictures).

Ask students to do exercise 2. Give them two minutes to scan and circle the color words. When the students have finished, check they have circled the color words in the text.

> **ANSWERS**
> Students should have circled the following color words: red, blue, yellow, green, brown, orange

Background information

To help students understand the optical illusion with the tiled cube better, ask them to cover up all the tiles surrounding the central orange tile in the shaded area so that only that tile is showing. Once they have done that, they will see that the tile looks brown and is the same color as the tile at the top in the center.

Close reading

Ask students to complete the exercise. Allow them some extra time so they can do the optical illusion activities. Draw students' attention to the words in the *Academic keywords* box and ask them to add them to their vocabulary notebooks.

> **ANSWERS**
> 1 Color is created by our brains.
> 2 Light plays a role in how our brain perceives images.
> 3 In the first illusion, the colors are the same.
> 4 Color is created according to our past experiences.
> 5 We all see the world in different ways.

Developing critical thinking

Check that students understand the term *optical illusion* and the expression *couldn't believe your eyes* before putting them into groups for the discussion. Afterwards, extend the discussion by asking students if they know of any other optical illusions.

Extra research task

Ask students to research optical illusions further. Ask them to find one online, by searching for *optical illusions*, and be prepared to describe it to other students in the next class.

READING 2 Colors and flags
Word count 497

Before you read

Background information

The use of flags originated from the need to identify sides in ancient battles. Pieces of cloth were tied to poles or spears, and held aloft so the soldiers could find their leaders. Emblems were also attached to the poles to help identify which side was which. It is thought that the Romans were the first to use cloth flags.

To lead in to the discussion, you could bring in a flag, or image of a flag, from your country. Ask: *Does anyone know whose flag this is? Why were flags invented? Who had the first flag? What colors are popular flag colors?* Then ask students to discuss the questions in the *Before you read* section with a partner.

> **ANSWER**
> White is used the most.

Global reading

Remind students of the scanning skill they learned in the last section. Give them three minutes to scan the article for the information about the flags.

> **ANSWERS**
> 1 Russia 4 Colombia
> 2 The United Nations 5 Mali
> 3 France 6 Kuwait

Close reading

1 Review the ways of organizing notes that students have already learned: organizing new words using nouns / verbs and adjectives / adverbs, using word maps, highlighting and annotating. Remind students about the highlighting and annotation skills they learned in unit 3. Ask students to highlight and annotate the text, or to take notes. Ask students to compare their notes and annotations. Who has the easiest notes to read and use as a study aid? Ask students to read the *Using a chart to organize your notes* box. Then, check comprehension. Ask: *What kind of information is a chart useful for organizing? Why is a chart useful in organizing comparing and contrasting information?*

2 Ask students to complete exercise 2 individually and then compare answers with a partner. When pairs have finished, ask them to share their answers with the class.

> **ANSWERS**
>
> | | Meaning 1 | Meaning 2 |
> |---|---|---|
> | Black | strength | determination |
> | White | peace | purity |
> | Blue | freedom | prosperity |
> | Red | blood | courage |
> | Green | earth | agriculture |
> | Yellow | sun | wealth |
> | Red, white, and blue | freedom | revolution |
> | Green, gold, and red | African unity | African identity |
> | Black, white, green, and red | Arab unity | different Arab dynasties |

3 Ask students to complete the sentences individually, then check the answers with the class.

> **ANSWERS**
> 1 symbolize the unity of a nation
> 2 "the opposite of red"
> 3 at least one of them appeared on the flag of every country of the world at the time
> 4 the race is finished
> 5 orange

Developing critical thinking

1 Ask students to discuss the questions in groups. Refer them to the words in the *Emotions* box to help with ideas. When they have finished, ask them to share their ideas with the whole class.

2 Remind students of the text *Is seeing really believing?* Ask them if they think there is a connection between this text and *Colors and flags*. Then ask them to discuss the questions in groups. Encourage them to use the words in the *Colors* box to give them ideas. When the students have finished, ask them to share their ideas with the class.

Extra research task

Ask students to research their flag, or another flag, to find out about the history and what the colors and symbols mean. They could do mini-presentations to share what they learned.

Students might also like to design their own flag. Put them into groups, and tell them that they are going to form a student group at their school or university. First, they must decide what the group is and what its values are. Then they can design a flag to symbolize their group.

Vocabulary skill

Ask students if they remember what a prefix is (unit 5) and have them give you some examples. Show students that just as we can add prefixes to the beginning of words, we can also add suffixes to the ends of words: *un + fair + ly → unfairly*. Ask: *What part of speech is* unfair? *What part of speech is* unfairly? *Do prefixes or suffixes change the part of speech?*

Remind students that they have already learned how to change adjectives into adverbs. Now ask them to read the *Adding suffixes to change verbs into nouns* box. Ask students to pay particular attention to the spelling. Be sure to check pronunciation.

As with choosing the correct prefix, it is difficult to know which suffix to choose. There are no firm rules for which suffix goes with which verb. Encourage students to use monolingual dictionaries to find the suffixes and to review them often.

1   Ask students to work individually to do the exercise. Be sure to check and drill pronunciation when checking the answers. Which syllable is the stressed syllable in the verb? In the noun?

ANSWERS

1 arrangement	4 information
2 appearance	5 depression
3 dependence	6 restriction

2   Ask students to work individually to do the exercise, then check the answers with the class.

ANSWERS

1 compose	4 conclude
2 manage	5 indicate
3 prefer	6 allow

3   Ask students to work individually to complete the sentences, then check the answers with the class.

ANSWERS

1 assistance	5 enjoyment
2 replacement	6 difference
3 composition	7 confusion
4 suggestion	8 appointment

Ask students what they think would be the best way to organize these new words and suffixes in their vocabulary notebook. Some ideas include: in word maps—write the suffix in the center and draw lines to connect to words that use that suffix; in charts—write the suffix at the top of the column and the words that use that suffix in the descending column; using color— color code the suffixes and words that use those suffixes.

EXTENSION ACTIVITY

Ask students to study the suffixes from this unit and the prefixes from unit 5, then host a team competition. Call out a word and ask the teams to add a suffix (or prefix) to the word and write it on a piece of paper. For example, ask them to change the verb *create* to a noun using a suffix. Ask the teams to swap papers to mark each other's work after you have called out ten words.

WRITING Describing colors

Writing skill

Background information

Students often make the mistake of writing sentence fragments even if English is their first language. This is possibly because students are accustomed to the informal style used in speaking where sentence fragments are not usually an issue. Writing complete sentences is a skill that all writers need to learn.

Asking students to identify the subject and verb in a sentence can help them realize when a sentence is incomplete. Also, recognizing words that signal dependent clauses can help students as well. Finally, students need to learn to recognize which is the dependent and which is the independent clause.

Introduce the topic by writing a sentence fragment on the board: *Because she likes flags.* Ask students if they think this is a good sentence and prompt them with questions such as: *Is there any information missing? Do we know the reason for this conclusion?* Ask students to think of a way to make the sentence feel more complete. Explain that this is a fragment, not a complete sentence. Ask students to read the *Writing complete sentences* box to learn about fragments.

When students have finished reading, ask them to discuss each fragment with a partner and decide why it is a fragment (i.e. Is it missing a subject? Is it missing a verb? etc.). Ask pairs to share their ideas with the class. Then ask students to underline the subject and verb in the sentences in the box. Point out that sentences 3 and 4 have two subjects and two verbs. Write these sentences on the board and illustrate the dependent and independent clauses:

[Since they adopted the U.N. flag in 1947], *it* has changed slightly.

It will not be easy [if the U.N. wants to change its flag.]

Point out that if the dependent clause comes first, a comma is needed in the sentence, but if it comes second, no comma is needed. Give some other examples to illustrate and practice.

1   Ask students to do the exercise. Encourage them to underline the subject once and the verb twice, to circle words that make a clause dependent, and to draw brackets around dependent clauses. As a follow-up activity, you could ask students to turn the fragments into sentences by adding whatever is needed to complete them.

ANSWERS
1 F [After we got home last night].
2 S Many flags in the Middle East contain the color green.
3 S Yemen's flag is three horizontal stripes of red, white, and black.
4 F [Because I study English].
5 S I cannot tell the difference between violet and purple.
6 S The colors in the sunset were beautiful.
7 F The color [that I like the most].
8 F [When I wake up every morning]

2 Ask the students to do the exercise individually, then check the answers with the class.

POSSIBLE ANSWER
The background on the South Korean flag is white because white is a traditional color of the Korean people. The blue and red circle in the center represents the origins of everything in the universe. The circle represents opposites, such as positive and negative, and night and day. The black lines around the circle represent the elements of fire, water, earth, wood, and metal. After you understand the symbolism behind this or any flag, you appreciate it more.

Grammar

Ask students what they know about count and noncount nouns, and have them give some examples. Then ask them to read the *Grammar* box to learn about the difference between the two. When they have finished reading, ask students to close their books and tell you what they learnt. How many of the seven categories of noncount nouns they can remember? Check that they understand that noncount nouns take a singular verb. Ask: *Do we say* coffee is *or* coffee are? *Why? Can we say* I have a luggage? *What about* three luggages? *Why not? What can I say if I have more than one?* (some luggage, three pieces of luggage).

Background information

Students may point out that you can say, *I'll have a coffee* or *He likes three sugars in his tea*. This is because, in these cases, we are actually referring to *cups* of coffee or *packets / teaspoons* of sugar—the container is understood from the context. Explore how to quantify noncount nouns (*a glass of milk, a slice of bread*), but only do this if your students are already comfortable with the count / noncount distinction. You may want to note the use of *some* before a count or noncount noun to denote "an amount of."

1 Ask students to complete the table in the *Grammar* box. Check the answers with the class.

ANSWERS
1 gasoline, water
2 cheese, gold
3 rice, salt
4 clothing, money
5 friendship, information
6 Arabic, engineering
7 heat, weather

2 Ask the students to do the exercise individually, then check the answers with the class.

ANSWERS
1 If you want me to make **cookies** [C], please buy some **flour** [N] and **sugar** [N].
2 The **weather** [N] was terrible on our **vacation** [C]. There was **rain** [N] every **day** [C].
3 Our **teacher** [C] said our **homework** [N] is not due until **Tuesday** [C].
4 At my **university** [C] lots of **students** [C] study **economics** [N].
5 Can you buy some **bread** [N], **cheese** [N], **fruit** [N], and **carrots** [C]?
6 This brown **furniture** [N] is not **wood** [N]. It is some kind of cheap **plastic** [N].

3 Ask students to do the exercise, then check the answers with the class.

ANSWERS
1 It takes a lot of patiences to teach children.
2 Iris never tells lies. She always tells the truths.
3 I need some advice on finding a job where I can use my Englishes.
4 The informations in these brochures is not accurate.
5 That department store sells both food and furnitures.
6 This meat needs salts and this sauce needs pepper.
7 The color red can represent bloods and courage.
8 The chemicals in the waters make it look orange.

WRITING TASK

Remind students about the discussion at the beginning of the unit about colors. Tell students they are going to write a paragraph about what three colors symbolize in their culture. Ask them to read the paragraph and follow the instructions. After they have finished, ask them which culture they think the writer is referring to (U.S. culture).

ANSWERS

Like many colors, yellow, blue, and green can have different meanings in different cultures. In my culture, yellow often means a lack of bravery. If you are afraid of something, you might be considered "yellow." We also have an expression "yellow journalism." This refers to journalism that is not always 100% true. Yellow is also used to mean slow down since it's the middle color on traffic lights. The color blue can represent sadness. For example, the expressions "to feel blue" and "to have the blues" mean to feel very sad. The color green can have several meanings in my culture. It can symbolize spring, growth, and nature. It can represent recycling and environmentalism. It can even represent money because our currency is green. Also, if you say someone is "green" it means that they don't have very much experience. I'm not sure why we say that!

Brainstorm, plan, and write

Ask students to follow the instructions to brainstorm using the word map. If students have trouble thinking of ideas, they could brainstorm with another student, or they could do an Internet search. They may look back at notes for ideas about expressions that they thought of at the beginning of the unit. Once they have written down their ideas, ask them to share them with another student. Encourage students to ask each other questions to enrich the information in their word maps.

Ask students to follow the instructions for planning. Some students may prefer to skip this stage and just start writing from the word map. Explain why planning is such an important skill, and encourage students to always include the planning stage.

When students have finished planning, ask them to write a 100–150 word paragraph. To ensure a clear context, ask them to give their paragraph a title: *Colors and their symbolism in* _____.

Share, rewrite, and edit

Ask students to exchange their paragraphs with a partner. Encourage students to use the Peer review checklist on page 109 when they are evaluating their partner's paragraph. Keep emphasizing that peer feedback is helpful to both the writer and the reader. The reader is practicing editing skills, and the writer gets feedback on things he/she might not have noticed. Praise students who give good feedback, and continue to encourage those students who struggle.

Ask students to rewrite and edit their paragraphs. Encourage them to take into consideration their partner's feedback when rewriting. Use the

photocopiable unit assignment checklist on page 94 to assess the students' paragraphs. If possible, have a consultation with students individually to talk about improvements from first to final drafts. If this is not possible, you could try using free, downloadable software which allows you to give oral feedback that the students can listen to at home.

Extra research task

Students might like to research color and how it can affect our moods. In groups, they could design a color scheme for a student union chill-out room. Encourage them to think about paint colors, furniture colors, etc. Have them present their ideas, saying why they have chosen the colors.

STUDY SKILLS Studying with others

Background information

Students may not be used to working in groups, or they may have varied opinions about group work. Working in groups is often required at school or university, at work, and within the community. Some common contexts are listed in this section. Group work can be very rewarding, but it requires members to work cooperatively. This section aims to raise student awareness of ways to work cooperatively and to help students evaluate their own strengths and weaknesses when studying with others.

Start by asking students when they are likely to work in groups. Ask them to compare their ideas to the contexts listed in the *Study skills* section. How many of these contexts do the students have experience with?

Ask students to think about the questions in the yellow box, and make notes if they want. Afterwards, ask them to discuss their ideas in a group. After several minutes, ask groups to give you highlights of what they discussed. You will most likely find that there is a link between what the students have said and the section on working cooperatively. Ask students to read this section to see how much the ideas in the section match their experience of working successfully in groups.

Ask students to complete the self-evaluation table individually. For aspects that they feel they are weak in, ask them to reflect on how they might improve. Students may want to compare answers and give each other advice, but don't insist on it.

As a follow-up, you could, as a class, draw up a groupwork code of conduct that everyone agrees to abide by in future class groupwork.

UNIT 8 EXTREMES

Reading	Finding similarities and differences Identifying the source
Vocabulary	Understanding compound words
Writing	Using transitions to add and emphasize information
Grammar	Expressing ability

Discussion point

Background information

The picture on page 77 shows a topographical map. The colors represent different elevations of Earth (e.g. mountains) and depths of the ocean. The colors get warmer as elevation increases—dark blue is the lowest elevation, and red is the highest elevation. Mountains are shown in yellow and red. If students are interested in exploring maps, you might like to show them Google Earth (earth.google.co.uk), which has 3-D maps of the Earth, moon, and Mars.

Ask the students to look at the picture and say what they think it is. Find out if they know which continents are shown and why the map has so many colors. Find out if they know what the mountainous ridge in the Atlantic Ocean is (the mid-Atlantic ridge) or the mountain range in South America (the Andes). Ask students to take the quiz, then discuss their answers with a partner. Photocopy and cut out the unit 8 *Useful language* page to provide some extra support. After students have finished their discussion, have them share their answers with the class.

ANSWERS
1 b   2 b   3 a

As a follow-up, find out if anyone has ever been to or would like to go to any of these places. You could also ask students what they know about other geographical extremes, using the unit title as a prompt (e.g. longest river, deepest lake, etc.). If students are struggling in their knowledge, you could assign them a research task. Give each student something to research for homework (e.g. longest river in the world or longest river in the country), or send them off for 20 minutes to find the answer in the library. Collate all the data into a chart and hang it in the room for the duration of the unit.

Vocabulary preview

Ask students to say what part of speech the words in the box are, using the suffixes as clues. Note that *dedicated* could be either an adjective or a past tense verb, though here it is an adjective. Ask students to predict what part of speech needs to go into each blank. Encourage them to use *an* and *to* as clues. Allow students to use their monolingual dictionaries to help them. When students have finished, check the answers with the class.

ANSWERS
1 firsthand	5 concerned
2 convince	6 operate
3 species	7 dedicated
4 eventually	8 investigate
	9 expedition

READING 1 Earth's final frontier

Word count 435

Background information

Culturally, the word *frontier* is loaded with meaning. In the age of discovery when Europeans were discovering new lands, *the frontier* had connotations of adventure, danger, freedom, discovery, and the possibility of finding wealth. For the Spanish, it was the Americas. For the Dutch, it was the Congo. People explored and "discovered" lands that they had never known before. A new "America" pushed westwards towards the Pacific Ocean into the western "frontier." Once every bit of land on Earth had been "discovered," attention turned to space as the "final frontier." But gradually, people started to realize that there were things to be discovered on this planet— oceans, lakes, caves, and volcanoes—and these became our frontiers. So, to say something is the "final frontier" means that it is the last place we can look to find adventure, danger, freedom, and possibly, wealth. It is our last place of discovery.

Before you read

Ask students what they think the title of the article means. Try to elicit the meaning of *frontier* by asking questions, e.g. *Are there any places left in the world to explore or has everything been discovered? What does a frontier have to do with exploring?* Refer students to the pictures, and ask them what the images have to do with the title. Ask: *Why is the ocean Earth's final frontier?* Ask them to work with a partner to discuss the questions, then ask some students to share their answers with the class.

Global reading

Ask students to predict what the article is about based on their discussion, the title, and the pictures. This section requires students to scan the article quickly for specific information. Remind students of the skill of scanning that they learned in the previous unit. Ask them to look at sentences 1–5 to find out what they need to scan the article for. They should notice that they are only looking for numbers. To add some variety and a competitive element to this activity, see who can get all the correct answers first.

When going over the answers, check that students can say the numbers correctly. You may want to point out that the decimal is said as "point," but the comma in larger numbers is not pronounced. Also, be aware that in some cultures decimals and commas are reversed (i.e. 26,7%; 12.000 miles) Your students may need to be made aware of the conventions in English.

> **ANSWERS**
> 1 11   4 7,000
> 2 26.7   5 11,033
> 3 2010

Close reading

> **Exam tip**
>
> Students may have to find similarities and differences, and fill in a chart or grid as an exam task. Recognizing similarities and differences also aids critical thinking.

Begin by asking students to look at the two pictures of *Alvin* and *Shinkai 6500* again and tell you what the differences between them are. Write *differences* on the board and list students' ideas under the heading. Then ask them what the similarities are. Write *similarities* on the board and list the students' ideas again. Refer students to the *Finding similarities and differences* box to learn more. When they have finished, ask them to close their books. See how many words they can remember that signal similarities and differences.

1 Ask students to highlight the similarities and differences in the article. For this activity, students need two highlighter colors. Ask them to share with another student if they don't have two colors. When students have finished, have them share ideas with the class.

> **ANSWERS**
> Highlighted words that indicate similarities: *like, also, neither, both*
> Highlighted words that indicate differences: *while, however, whereas, but*

> **Background information**
>
> A Venn diagram is a type of graphic organizer that is used extensively in education because it graphically shows connections and relations between ideas. Venn diagrams can help students understand the relationships between ideas and are also useful in helping to organize writing. In the Venn diagram in this unit, students are asked to write what is unique about *Alvin* in the left-hand side of the left circle, what is unique about *Shinkai 6500* in the right-hand side of the right circle, and the properties they share in the central section where the two circles intersect.

You may need to introduce students to the concept of the Venn diagram if they have never encountered one before. Using the ideas generated prior to exercise 1, draw a Venn diagram on the board and list the differences in the outer parts of the circles and the similarities in the part where the two circles intersect. Ask: *Why is this information on this side? Why is this information on the other side? Why is this information in the center? Can I put this information in the center? Why not?* You could extend students' knowledge of Venn diagram use by talking about what other subjects they might be useful for.

2 Ask students to complete the Venn diagram. When they have finished, check the answers with the class. Students should note the words in the *Academic keywords* box and record them in their vocabulary notebooks. You might want to point out that *record* has two pronunciations, depending on whether it is a verb or a noun: /rɪˈkɔrd/(v) and /ˈrekərd/(n).

> **ANSWERS**
>
>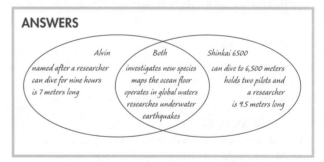
>
> *Alvin* — named after a researcher / can dive for nine hours / is 7 meters long
> *Both* — investigates new species / maps the ocean floor / operates in global waters / researches underwater earthquakes
> *Shinkai 6500* — can dive to 6,500 meters / holds two pilots and a researcher / is 9.5 meters long

Developing critical thinking

> **SUPPORTING CRITICAL THINKING**
>
> Always encourage students to give reasons to support their opinions. In this unit, students have to think laterally about some of the issues presented in the text. Encourage them to use some of the information they have learned to support their opinions in a more academic way. For example, a reason for thinking that exploring the ocean floor is a good idea might be because scientists can learn about new species or find out about underwater earthquakes in order to prevent disasters caused by them.

Divide the class into groups to discuss the questions. Refer them to the words in the *Dangers* box for question 2. Be sure to encourage students to give reasons to support their opinions. When they have finished, ask them to share their ideas with the class.

EXTENSION ACTIVITY

You could ask students to design a way that *Alvin* or *Shinkai 6500* could be used to investigate a body of water in their country. Alternatively, you could ask students to research other methods scientists use to explore underwater (e.g. sonar) or other bodies of water that have been explored (e.g. Loch Ness). Also, take a look at the *National Geographic* website for videos and pictures related to underwater exploration (e.g. video: *Cameron dive first attempt in over 50 years*—they took a submersible to the Mariana Trench).

READING 2 Super Sherpa

Word count 560

Background information

Although for most people the term *Sherpa* conjures the image of a Himalayan guide, *Sherpa* actually refers to an ethnic group of people who live in the Himalayan mountain range in Nepal. Originally they were nomadic and may have come from Tibet. Because they are known for their mountaineering skills, they have been hired as guides on expeditions in the Himalayas and up to Mount Everest. Tenzing Norgay was the Sherpa who accompanied Sir Edmund Hillary in 1953. They were the first people known to reach the summit of Mount Everest.

Before you read

Ask students to look at the picture on page 80 and discuss the questions with a partner. Follow up by asking some students to share their ideas with the class.

POSSIBLE ANSWER

The picture shows trash on a mountain. It was taken on Mount Everest. The trash was left there by people who had climbed the mountain.

Global reading

To introduce the idea of different sources, ask students what kinds of things they read either in their native language, in English, or another language. Brainstorm as a class and write these on the board. Ask students if there is any difference in the type of writing in, say, a newspaper and a novel. (For example, a newspaper would have information whereas a novel would have a story.) You could ask students to choose two types of writing and make a Venn diagram, as in the last section, showing how they are alike and how they are different.

Then ask students to read the *Identifying the source* box. Make sure students understand what *layout* means, e.g. a newspaper has a headline and is printed in columns. Ask them to skim the article in two minutes and decide what the source is. Ask them to tell you what clues they used to discover the source.

ANSWER

3 Environmental newsmagazine

Close reading

1 Remind students about the skill they learned about in unit 5—identifying the main idea and supporting details. Ask: *What is a main idea? What is a supporting detail?* Then ask students to do exercise 1 individually. Have pairs compare answers, then check the answers together as a class before moving on to the next exercise.

ANSWERS

1 M	5 M
2 S	6 S
3 M	7 M
4 S	

2 Ask students to write the answers in complete sentences. When students have finished, check the answers with the class.

ANSWERS

1 They're known for their ability to carry heavy loads for long distances at high altitudes.
2 He climbed Mount Everest for the first time in 1990.
3 The sign said, "Stop Climate Change."
4 He founded the Apa Sherpa Foundation, which is dedicated to improving the education and economic development of the Nepalese people.
5 He is known as the "Super Sherpa" for the ease with which he climbs mountains.

Find out what the students know about Sherpas. You may want to give them more information about the Sherpa people, where they live, and why, to many people, the term *Sherpa* means *guide* or *porter*.

3 Remind students of the skill of making inferences that they learned in unit 4. Ask them to do the exercise, then check the answers with the class.

ANSWER

Statements that you can infer: 2, 3, 5

Ask students to think back to unit 1 where they read about heroes. Ask: *Do you think Apa is a hero? Why or why not?*

Developing critical thinking

You might want to discuss the following questions as a class before putting students into groups for the discussion. Ask: *What message is Apa trying to get across to the world? What evidence does he use to support his message about climate change?*

1 Ask groups of students to discuss the questions. Encourage them to use the *Characteristics* box for question 1. To support their discussion, ask them to make a word map of Apa Sherpa's characteristics. You could also ask them to think of at least five more ways he could get his message to a wider audience. Invite students to share their ideas with the class before moving on to exercise 2.

Extra research task

Students might like to research Apa Sherpa further. If they search for *Apa Sherpa*, they will find several sites featuring him, including his own website and his foundation, the Apa Sherpa Foundation. After finding out more about him, students could send him a message—possibly on his website via *Contact*.

2 Remind students of the text *Earth's final frontier*. Ask them if they think there is a connection between this text and *Super Sherpa*. To support critical thinking and to help students organize information, ask them to discuss their ideas and then draw a Venn diagram comparing Apa and researchers in submersibles. Then have them discuss the questions in groups. Encourage them to use the words in the *Think about* box to help.

Vocabulary skill

Students have already seen the word *compound* in unit 4, where they learned to write compound sentences. Ask students if they remember what a compound sentence is, and elicit *two sentences put together to make one sentence*. Ask them what they think a compound word is. See if they can think of any examples (e.g. *sunflower, butterfly*). Ask them to read the *Understanding compound words* box to find four more. Then ask them which pattern the words in the box follow (i.e. *sunset* = noun + verb; *marine biologist* = adjective + noun).

1 Ask students to look back at the two texts from this unit to find the answers for this exercise. Check the answers with the class.

ANSWERS

1 mother ship	6 primary school
2 shipwreck	7 uphill
3 earthquake	8 mountain climber
4 ocean floor	9 firsthand
5 hometown	10 climate change

2 Ask students to find the word that makes the compound word when combined with the first word in bold. To extend this activity further, ask students to think of, or find in their dictionary, at least two more compound nouns beginning with the word in bold. You could also do this as a class using the *Macmillan Dictionary* online on the projector (e.g. *base camp, base jumping; stoplight, pit stop; workshop, work experience; lunch break, coffee break; overkill, overall*).

ANSWERS

1 baseball	4 breakfast
2 stop sign	5 overtime
3 workout	

3 Ask students to work individually to do the exercise. Use the *Macmillan Dictionary* online (http://www.macmillandictionary.com) could also be a useful resource for students doing this exercise. When students have finished, have them share their ideas with the class.

EXTENSION ACTIVITY

Give each student ten slips of paper. Ask them to write the first part of compound words on the slips—one word per slip. Collect the slips, mix them up, and then give pairs 20 slips facedown. Tell them that Student A is going to be the timekeeper, and Student B is going to turn over slips of paper one by one and make a compound word for each. He/She must keep doing this for 30 seconds until Student A calls "time's up." Then pairs switch roles. The student who turned over the most slips of paper and made the most compound words "wins." Be sure to model the activity first so that students understand what to do.

WRITING Giving your opinion

Writing skill

Lead in to the topic of transitions by writing *trans ...* on the board. Ask students to tell you the rest of the word. They will probably say *transport*. Ask them what *transport* means (to take something from one place to another). Tell them that *trans* is a prefix (unit 5) meaning *across, beyond, through*. Ask them what they think *transnational* and *transatlantic* mean. Tell students that they are going to learn about using transitions in their writing. Find out if they know what a transition is, and then give them some examples of transitions they do know: *and, but, in addition*. Ask students what they think a transition does. Hopefully they will say that it links two ideas or two sentences together. Emphasize that transitions are like the glue that holds things together. Transitions in writing make the paragraph stick together.

1 Ask students to read the *Using transitions to add and emphasize information* box. Check their comprehension of *emphasize*. Highlight transitions that can begin a sentence and which need a comma (*above all, in fact, in addition, moreover*), and those that cannot begin a sentence (*and, as well*). Ask students to do the exercise individually, then check the answers with the class.

> **ANSWERS**
> 1 There are many in the Caribbean Sea as well.
> 2 Moreover, a sea is surrounded by land.
> 3 In addition, it is the largest by volume.
> 4 It is also one of the most shallow.
> 5 The blue whale is the largest and heaviest mammal.

Exam tip

In writing for exams, students will be graded on how well their paragraphs hold together. Cohesion is aided by the use of transitions, so emphasize to students how important it is to use transitions in their writing when taking an exam.

2 Ask the students to complete the sentences using the words in the box, then check the answers with the class.

> **ANSWERS**
> 1 clearly / certainly   3 clearly / certainly
> 2 Above all   4 In fact

Grammar

Background information

Students have already seen the modal *should* for giving advice. *Can* and *be able to* express ability in both the present and past tense. (N.B. *Can* is not used in the future, but *will be able to* could be considered the future of *can*.) Students will need to be aware that *can* and *could* are not conjugated, but *be* in *be able to* is.

The other issue that arises with *can* and *cannot*, or *can't*, is pronunciation. *Can* is unstressed in sentences and sounds like /kən/. *Can't*, on the other hand, is stressed and the full vowel is pronounced: /kænt/. In the short answer or when the word is emphasized, both are stressed: *Yes, I can* /kæn/. *Cannot* is used in written language, especially in academic or formal writing. Few people use *cannot* in speech.

Begin by asking students questions about their abilities. Ask: *Can you ski? Are you able to swim? When you were little, could you tie your shoes? Were you able to send a text message when you were little?*, etc. Tell students you are asking about their abilities. Write the sentence frames on the board with a timeline:

Past ability		Ability now
←--------------------	--------------------	-------------------- →
Could you …? = Were you able to …?		Can you …? = Are you able to …?

1 Invite students to ask each other some questions about their past ability and their ability now. After a few minutes, ask them to read the *Grammar* box. Check their comprehension, then ask them to do exercise 1.

> **ANSWERS**
> 1 cannot   4 could
> 2 could not   5 can
> 3 am not able to 6 cannot

2 Ask students to rewrite the sentences individually, then check the answers with the class.

> **POSSIBLE ANSWERS**
> 1 I cannot swim.
> 2 Ben was not able to make it to the top of the mountain.
> 3 Kamal is able to name over a hundred types of tropical fish.
> 4 My brother and I were able to go camping by ourselves as kids.
> 5 Richard could not win his first swimming race last month.

WRITING TASK

Tell students they are going to write a paragraph about sports. Ask them to read the paragraph and follow the instructions. After they have finished, ask them if they agree or disagree with the opinion in the paragraph.

> **ANSWERS**
> Team sports such as baseball and volleyball <u>can teach</u> us a lot about life. First, sports <u>can show</u> us that we need to work hard. For example, we may need to pace ourselves [and] have endurance to achieve our aims. [In addition], practice is important if we want to be good at a sport. I <u>couldn't play</u> basketball well in high school, but I kept practicing and now I <u>can play</u> well. Second, sports clearly prepare students for the real world. Players learn how to work together and get along. They learn how to solve problems [as well]. [In fact], all of these are essential skills for working in any business or organization. Third, sports [also] teach us about failing. Winning isn't everything. Every game or sport will have a winner and a loser, and sports <u>are able to teach</u> us that it's OK to lose sometimes, if you try your best. [Moreover], we often learn more from our failures than our successes.

Brainstorm, plan, and write

In groups of three or four, ask students to read the opinions about sports and discuss which one they agree with and why they agree with it. Ask them to write the opinion they chose in the first row of the table, and then write three reasons that support that opinion. Ask them to share their reasons with another student who should evaluate if the reason supports the opinion or not. Students may find it hard to find reasons to support their opinion, so allow lots of peer interaction and make yourself available to give help and advice.

Ask students to plan carefully. They may wish to use the opinions in the box as their topic sentence, or they may wish to paraphrase it.

When students have finished planning, ask them to write a 100–150 word paragraph. For the final draft of this unit's assignment, you may wish to ask students to type and print it out or email it to you following the *Study skills* section, which talks about using computers for effective study.

Share, rewrite and edit

Ask students to exchange their paragraphs with a partner. Encourage students to use the Peer review checklist on page 109 when they are evaluating their partner's paragraph.

Ask students to rewrite and edit their paragraphs. Encourage them to take into consideration their partner's feedback when rewriting.

Use the photocopiable unit assignment checklist on page 95 to assess the students' paragraphs.

STUDY SKILLS Using computers for effective study

Background information

We tend to think that just because children grow up with technology they automatically know how to use it effectively. You may find that your students are able to navigate the web or use social networking sites with ease, but they may not know how to use a word processor effectively. Put a blank document up on the screen and show students how to use the spell checker, grammar function, the thesaurus and dictionary function, how to change the font type and size, and how to bold and underline text. In addition, show them how to use the word count function and how to print. These are the basics students will need to type a paper to turn in for class.

Begin with a quick discussion of computers: how students use them, which system they use, and if they use word processing programs. Ask students to discuss the questions with a partner and then share their answers with the class.

Scenario

Ask students to do this exercise with a partner. Elicit whole-class feedback from one pair and check to see if the rest of the class agrees.

POSSIBLE ANSWER

Ingrid drafts and edits her work, and she checks her spelling and grammar. However, Ingrid would save a lot of time if she used the computer because she would not have to write out her assignment again. She could also use the computer spell and grammar check functions.

Consider it

Ask students to work in pairs to read and discuss the tips. Once students have discussed the tips and added more, you may want to show them how to do some of the things on the computer using the projector.

Over to you

Ask students to discuss the questions with a partner. Monitor the activity and elicit feedback. As a follow-up, students could draw a Venn diagram to compare and contrast the benefits of using traditional study methods (e.g. notebooks, books, pen and paper) with the benefits of using a computer.

At the end of this lesson, use the video resource *Pushing the limits*. It is located in the Video resources section of the Digibook. Alternatively, remind the students about the video resource so they can do this at home.

UNIT 9 LIFE

Reading	Summarizing Identifying reasons
Vocabulary	Finding the correct definition of a word
Writing	Using transitions to sequence events
Grammar	The simple past tense

Discussion point

Begin by referring students to the picture. Ask them if it is related to the title of the unit, *Life*. Why or why not? Ask them to discuss the questions with a partner they do not usually work with. Photocopy and cut out the unit 9 *Useful language* page to provide extra support. Ask several pairs to share their answers with the class. You could draw students' attention to the compound words *childhood* and *adulthood* as a reminder of what they learned in unit 8.

Cultural awareness

It might be interesting to briefly find out if the stages listed correspond to the stages of life in the students' cultures. In some cultures, children are one year old when they are born. Do the ages listed correspond to the same stages in the students' cultures? Are there more or fewer stages? At what age can people get married / vote / retire?

Vocabulary preview

Ask students to use their monolingual dictionaries to find out about the part of speech, pronunciation, meaning, and/or synonyms of the words in the box. Ask them to think about what part of speech goes in each blank. As a link back to the *Study skills* section in unit 8, you could ask the students to use the thesaurus function on the computer to find synonyms.

ANSWERS
1 adolescent	5 capability
2 familiar	6 resistant
3 Discard	7 transition
4 technical	8 sustain

READING 1 Coming of age

Word count 475

Background information

Coming of age rites of passage are just one example of transition rites people of all cultures go through in their life. French ethnographer Arnold van Gennep observed that rites of passage are universal and only differ across cultures in the ways they are celebrated. Rites of passage are transitions in which people cross from one social status to another—from childhood to adulthood, for example. Predictably, biological rites of passage occur at significant periods in a person's life: birth, toddler, child, puberty, young adult, mature adult, senior, and death*, though there may be many other periods in between and not all people will go through all periods (e.g. marriage and parenthood).

In modern society, rites of passage may be celebrated less traditionally or not at all. In the UK, for example, few families would celebrate their child's transition into puberty. Similarly, different families will have different celebrations for the transition into adulthood at the age of 18.

* In Akan society, death marks the transition from elder to ancestor, though not all elders have the honor of becoming ancestors.

Before you read

1 Ask students what the pictures on page 88 show. Ask: *Is the first haircut an important step in someone's life? What about for the parents of the boy? What about the boy in the second picture?* Explain that this is an important *rite of passage* for many people. Ask them what they think the phrase means. Refer to the examples in the *Rites of passage* box to help students understand the concept, then ask them to discuss the questions with a partner. Ask if there are any rites of passage that are important in their cultures that are not listed.

2 Ask students to look at the title and pictures on page 89 and predict what the text will be about. Ask them to predict what *coming of age* means, and then figure it out from the text when they do the *Global reading* exercise.

Global reading

Give students two minutes to skim the text to find out if their predictions were correct.

ANSWER
The text will be about the adolescent and teen years.

Background information

Some students may still be unable to skim the entire text in the time limit provided. This could be because they are trying to read every word. They also may be stopping when they encounter a word they don't know. Good readers skim read in clumps of words, not every word. To help students skim faster, ask them to move their finger along the row of words quickly as they read, but not to stop the finger movement. Ask them to reflect afterwards if this helped them to skim read the text more quickly.

Close reading

Exam tip

Recognizing main points and summarizing them are important skills for students to develop, especially if they plan to use English in university studies. In exams, students may have to match headings containing key points with paragraphs that contain the key details, or they might have to fill in blanks in a summary with information from a text. The close reading activity is just such a task.

Summaries are often used in university settings to test if students have understood the main ideas of a reading or lecture. Summary writing is a good way to prepare students for university studies where they will have to understand the main ideas of texts, and then write about them in essays and reports.

SUPPORTING CRITICAL THINKING

Being able to identify main points and the details that support those points can aid critical thinking, especially when trying to follow an author's line of argument.

To introduce the idea of summarizing, ask students to think of a good book or a good movie. Ask them to quickly tell their partner about the main points of the story or movie. Give them a few minutes to switch roles, and then tell them that they have been summarizing. Ask them what they think it means, then refer them to the *Summarizing* box to check their ideas. When they have finished, check students' comprehension of what a summary includes. Ask: *Does it include main ideas? Does it include unimportant information?* Emphasize that summaries need to be in the students' own words and must not contain any information that is not in the original text.

Ask the students to annotate the text, then ask them to close their books and, with a partner, summarize the key points of the article. Then ask them to complete the summary in the book. Afterwards, ask them how similar their oral summary was to the summary in the book. It is OK if the summaries are slightly different.

ANSWERS

1 adult	5 driver's license
2 passage	6 ceremony
3 preparation	7 diving
4 recognized	8 responsibility

As a follow-up, you may want to have a discussion about the different rites of passage in the text. Are there any other ceremonies in other cultures that students know about?

Draw students' attention to the words in the *Academic keywords* box and ask them to add them to their vocabulary notebook.

Developing critical thinking

The ceremonies in the text mark the rite of passage into adulthood. If students are all from the same culture, then for question 1 you might compare the students' culture with the cultures in the text. For example, ask: *When is someone considered an adult in Vanuatu? And in your culture?* Alternatively, you could talk about your own culture. Draw students' attention to the *Life events* box for question 3.

Extra research task

Students may be interested in researching the rites of passage listed on page 88 in other cultures. Try to get students to focus on some of the traditions that different cultures have. You might want to deter students from judging "bizarre" rites of passage, though. Ask them to maintain a spirit of different, yet equal.

READING 2 Gardening 380 kilometers above Earth

Word count 502

Background information

Growing plants on a space station seems a logical idea. After all, they produce oxygen and food needed for the astronauts living there. Another reason to grow plants in space is to provide food for future human colonies on the moon or planets such as Mars. Scientists are studying ways to grow plants without the need for bio-rich soil—something that has not (yet) been found anywhere but on Earth. Aeroponics systems (growing plants in moist, nutrient-rich air) have been the subject of experimentation since the middle of the twentieth century and have been commercially used since 1983. Space gardening has opened up a world of ideas for growing plants in inhospitable places here on Earth, too. Urban plant walls allow plants to be grown vertically in places where there is no soil. Similarly, arid places can make use of aeroponics for growing, since very little water is used.

Before you read

Introduce the topic of gardening. Ask: *Does anyone have a garden? Do you grow flowers, or fruits and vegetables? What do plants need to grow? What problems are there when growing plants?*

Ask students to comment on the title: *Gardening 380 kilometers above Earth*. Then ask them to work with a partner to discuss the questions.

Global reading

Remind slower readers to use their finger to follow the words if it helped in the previous reading. Give them about two minutes to skim the text before choosing the best sub-title.

> **ANSWER**
> **3** Growing plants in space

Close reading

> **Background information**
>
> This section requires students to find key information and then summarize it. At this level, students may feel more comfortable copying sentences from the text, but encourage them to use their own words. You could ask students to write the summary with a partner. Allow plenty of time, as students will need to discuss and agree on key points and how to summarize them. If you have an overhead projector, you could ask students to write on overhead transparencies so that all the summaries could be shared with the class. Try to build students' confidence by giving them lots of positive encouragement when they write the summaries. At this stage, it is less important how grammatically accurate the summaries are, and more important that the students are using their own words and identifying main ideas. It is probably best not to identify the "best" summary in the class, but to find something good about each attempt.

1 Ask students to read the text, and highlight and annotate it carefully. To help avoid copying in the summary, students could be encouraged to take good notes and write the summary from the notes rather than from the original text.

> **POSSIBLE ANSWER**
> Astronauts are growing plants in space. It is expensive to send anything to space so this saves money. Plants are a renewable food source, and they improve air quality. There are some challenges with growing plants in space, especially the lack of gravity and the need for soil. However, the use of fans and special gels are helping overcome the challenges. Scientists are also working on the plants. They are breeding them to grow more efficiently and be disease resistant. These innovations may also improve life on Earth.

> **Exam tip**
>
> Identifying reasons is a skill that may be tested on exams in order to assess students' ability to recognize relationships and connections between ideas. Students may be asked to match the reason to a particular cause, event, or action.

2 Ask students to circle the words in the text that signal reasons. Then ask them to do the exercise. When the students have finished, check the answers with the class.

> **ANSWERS**
> 1 They wanted familiar foods to ease their transition to foreign lands.
> 2 The trips can be very long, and it is expensive to send anything into space.
> 3 They use carbon dioxide and produce oxygen.
> 4 It stays around the plants because of the lack of gravity.
> 5 They use gels because soil is too heavy to send to space.

3 Remind the students of the skill of pronoun referencing they learnt in unit 1. Then ask them to read the text again to work out what the words in bold refer to. Check the answers with the class.

> **ANSWERS**
> 1 a early explorers   b early explorers
> 2 a the oxygen   b the plants
> 3 a special gels   b water

As an alternative, you could divide pairs into A, B, and C groupings and ask each group to make a word map of ideas following the discussion. A groups make a word map of reasons astronauts grow plants in space; B groups make a Venn diagram of how plants in space and on Earth might differ / how they might be the same; C groups make a word map of the challenges of growing plants in space. After a few minutes, ask all of the A, B, and C groups to share ideas. Finally, group students into new groups with someone from A, B, and C in each new group to summarize their ideas.

Developing critical thinking

1 Ask the students to discuss the questions in a group. For the first question, ask them to discuss the traits in the *Personality traits* box. Also, draw their attention to the words in the *Academic keywords* box. When the students have finished, ask them to share their ideas with the class.

2 Remind students of the text *Coming of age*. Ask them if they think there is a connection between this text and *Gardening 380 kilometers above Earth*. Then ask them to discuss the questions in exercise 2 in groups. Draw their attention to the *Think about* box to help with their discussions. When they have finished, ask them to share their ideas with the class.

This is a good place in the lesson to use the video resource *Saving the bees*. It is located in the Video resources section of the Digibook. Alternatively, remind students about the video resource so they can do this at home.

Vocabulary skill

Tell students they are going to work on dictionary skills. Find out what they find difficult about using a monolingual dictionary. You could do a Venn diagram to compare and contrast the advantages and disadvantages of monolingual and bilingual dictionaries. Students may say that they don't understand the vocabulary in the definition in monolingual dictionaries. They might point out that the downside of using a bilingual dictionary is that they only get one translation or no examples. Give them encouragement—the more words they are exposed to, the more vocabulary they are learning. Reassure them that as they progress in their language studies, using a monolingual dictionary will get easier! Maybe a good compromise is to use both in tandem—look up the word in the monolingual dictionary to find out a variety of definitions, pronunciation, part of speech, and examples, and use a bilingual dictionary or translator afterwards, if needed.

1 Ask students to read the *Finding the correct definition of a word* box. Make sure they understand that definition 1 goes with sentence 1 and definition 2 goes with sentence 2. Ask the students to do the exercise individually, then check the answers with the class.

> **ANSWERS**
> a 2   b 3   c 1

2 Ask the students to do the exercise individually, then check the answers with the class.

> **ANSWERS**
> a 2   b 3   c 5   d 1   e 4

WRITING Describing a memorable day

Writing skill

To introduce the topic of sequencing events, write some words related to your daily routine on the board in random order: *wake up, get up, take a shower, brush your teeth, eat breakfast, go running, drink coffee,* etc. Ask students to work with a partner to put the actions in the sequence they think you do them. After three minutes, check their ideas. Write the correct sequence on the board, and as you do, orally use sequencing transitions: *Yes, so, <u>first</u> I wake up, and <u>then</u> I get up and go running. <u>After that</u> I take a shower …* Next, point out that this is the sequence of events in your daily routine. Check that students understand that *sequence = order* or *series* of when things happen. Ask them to tell you some of the words you used to show what happened when, and write them on the board. Then ask students to read the information in the *Using transitions to sequence events* box. Check that they understand the differences between the different sequencers before moving on to the practice exercises.

1 Ask students to do the exercise individually, then check the answers with the class.

> **ANSWERS**
> 1 after; Meanwhile; later
> 2 When; Before; at the same time
> 3 First; Second; Before
> 4 once; While; as soon as

2 Ask students to do the exercise individually, then ask them to share their ideas with the class.

Grammar

To extend practice with sequencers and introduce the idea of past tense, ask students to tell their partner what they did over the past weekend. Ask them to say what they did first, next, etc. As they talk, monitor and write down verbs you hear—either correctly in the past or not. After four minutes, stop the activity and write some of these verbs on the board. Ask students to tell you what tense the words are in. For any in the present tense, ask them what they think the past tense is. Ask them which tense should be used when talking about what they did the previous weekend or day. Refer students to the *Grammar* box. The *Grammar* box also lists four situations in which the past tense is used. Check students' comprehension by asking which of the four situations applied when they talked about their past weekend.

> **Background information**
>
> This would be a good opportunity to make sure students know the correct pronunciation of the -*ed* ending for regular verbs. The rule is: for verbs ending in a voiceless consonant sound, (f, k, p, s, x), the -*ed* ending sounds like /t/; for verbs ending in a voiced consonant sound, (b, g, j, l, m, n, q, r, v, w, y, z, and vowels) the -*ed* ending sounds like /d/; for verbs ending in a *d* or *t*, the -*ed* ending sounds like /ɪd/ and adds an extra syllable.
>
> | /t/ | /d/ | /ɪd/ |
> |---|---|---|
> | walk – /wɔkt/ | try – /traɪd/ | taste – /teɪstɪd/ |
> | hope – /həʊpt/ | jog – /dʒɑgd/ | need – /niːdɪd/ |
>
> It is important to point out that it is the final sound before the -*ed* ending and <u>not</u> the final letter that determines the pronunciation. To learn how to pronounce the past tense correctly, students need to understand the idea of voiced and voiceless sounds, and syllables. Mention that it is the /ɪd/ ending with the extra syllable that is most likely to cause problems. If a student doesn't pronounce the extra syllable in *needed* or *tasted*, then the verb would not be clearly understood as past.

Ask students to put their hand on their throats and say the soft sound /k/ (not /kə/!). Ask them if they feel anything. They shouldn't. Now ask them to say the sound /g/. Ask them if they feel anything. They should feel a vibration. Go back to /k/ and /g/ again so that students can feel the difference. Tell them that when they say /k/, they don't use their voice, but when they say /g/, they do. Write *voiceless* and *voiced* on the board, and write /k/ and /g/ in the correct column. Try the same with some of the other sounds, and ask students to say which column they belong in. Ask them if *walk* ends in a voiced or voiceless sound, and show them how the past tense -*ed* ending sounds like voiceless /t/ because the /k/ is voiceless. Do the same for the voiced -*ed*. Give some examples of verbs and ask them to say them with their hand on their throat and put them in the correct column. Introduce the idea of words ending in the /t/ and /d/ sound. Show students how the past tense ending is not clear if we say /teɪstt/ or /niːdd/. Say the word *taste*, while clapping, and ask how many syllables it has (one). Then do the same with *tasted*, and ask how many syllables it has (two). Repeat this with *need* and other verbs ending in the /t/ or /d/ sound.

1 Ask students to do the exercise individually, then check the answers with the class. When going over the answers, make sure that students pronounce the regular past tense verbs with the correct -*ed* ending.

> **ANSWERS**
> 1 got; had   4 retired; worked
> 2 did not go; broke   5 told; did not lose;
> 3 bought; shared   turned

2 Ask the students to do the exercise individually, then check the answers with the class.

> **ANSWERS**
> 1 felt   5 did not find
> 2 took   6 studied
> 3 stood   7 held
> 4 got   8 screamed

WRITING TASK

Cultural awareness

In the U.S., graduating from high school at the age of 18 is a big rite of passage. The paragraph gives a good overview of some key points of the graduation, and students may have seen the ceremony in American movies. Other countries may not celebrate graduating from high school. In the U.K., for example, there is no formal celebration after students finish their A-level exams.

Ask students to read the paragraph and work individually to do the exercise. When they have finished, check the answers with the class.

ANSWERS

I remember my high school graduation very well. Besides my immediate family, a lot of my aunts, uncles, and cousins <u>came</u> to the ceremony. I <u>put</u> on my graduation gown and cap and we all <u>drove</u> to the ceremony. It <u>didn't last</u> very long. Some people <u>gave</u> speeches and <u>then</u> they <u>presented</u> awards. We all just <u>sat</u> there quietly <u>during</u> all that. <u>Next</u>, they <u>handed</u> us our diplomas. <u>While</u> we <u>stood</u> in line to receive them, my mother <u>took</u> a lot of photos and my brother <u>tried</u> to make me laugh. I think my mom <u>cried</u> a little. <u>Once</u> I <u>got</u> my diploma, I <u>felt</u> really fantastic. <u>After</u> everyone <u>had</u> their diplomas, we all <u>threw</u> our graduation caps up in the air. That's a fun tradition. <u>Later,</u> at home, my friends and family <u>gave</u> me cards and presents. I <u>had</u> a great day.

Brainstorm, plan, and write

Give students some time to brainstorm, then ask them to share their ideas with a partner. Encourage pairs to ask each other questions and give each other more ideas about what they could write. Then ask them to fill in the chart.

The chart will list the basic information, but encourage students to add details or possibly reasons to enrich their descriptions. For example, they might add information about the weather, how they were feeling, or what they were wearing.

When students have finished planning, ask them to write a 100–150 word paragraph.

Share, rewrite, and edit

Ask students to exchange their paragraphs with a partner. Encourage students to ask questions about the information in each other's paragraph and to help each other add more details as needed. Encourage students to use the Peer review checklist on page 109 when they are evaluating their partner's paragraph.

Ask students to rewrite and edit their paragraphs. Encourage them to take into consideration their partner's feedback when rewriting.

Use the photocopiable unit assignment checklist on page 96 to assess the students' paragraphs.

STUDY SKILLS Making the most of your dictionary

Getting started

Bring in a variety of monolingual dictionaries for students to look at. Some dictionaries are for advanced students, but others are suitable for lower level students. Dictionary choice is a personal preference, so allow students to look at several. There are also several online dictionaries that students could use.

Remind students of the dictionary skill they looked at earlier in the unit, and tell them they are going to learn more tips for using dictionaries. Ask them to discuss the questions with a partner they do not usually work with.

Scenario

Ask students to do this exercise with a partner. Elicit whole-class feedback from one pair and check to see if the rest of the class agrees.

POSSIBLE ANSWER

Kwame uses the guidewords to find words quickly and looks for the correct definition. However, he does not study the pronunciation.

Consider it

Divide students into three groups. Ask students in group A to read tips 1–2, group B tips 3–4, and group C tips 5–6. You may need to give groups A and B some help by showing them the introduction and the guidewords in a dictionary. Once they have looked at the dictionaries, tell students to summarize the tips for classmates who did not read about them. Give students a couple of minutes to think about what to say, and then ask them to close their books. Regroup students so that there is at least one A, one B, and one C student in each new grouping. Ask students in each group to summarize the tips for each other. See if they can come up with any other tips.

Follow up the discussion by having everyone look in their dictionaries to find the introduction. Get them to compare the information there. Also, get them to find the guidewords and compare pictures, illustrations, etc. for each dictionary. Based on their study of dictionaries, ask students to decide which one they like best!

Over to you

Ask students to discuss the questions with a partner. Monitor the activity and elicit feedback.

EXTENSION ACTIVITY

Have a dictionary relay. Divide the class into A and B pairs with one dictionary per pair. Ask all the A's to come to the front and give all of them the same word. They must go back to their partner and, together, look up the word and provide some additional information (e.g. part of speech, example sentence, definition, etc.). They must write this on a piece of paper to bring back to you. When you have checked it is correct, you give them the next word. If it is not correct, they have to go back and correct it. Do this three times, then ask Student A to stay at the desk and Student B to come forward. The "winning" team is the one that gets through all six words first.

Reading	Sequencing
	Reading charts and graphs
Vocabulary	Using collocations
Writing	Using parallel structure
Grammar	Future forms

Discussion point

Ask students what kind of place they see in the picture on page 97. Ask them to say what they think the factory produces, if it is a modern factory, why the people are wearing masks and caps on their hair, etc. Then ask them to discuss the questions with a partner, using the sentence frames to help them get started. Photocopy and cut out the unit 10 *Useful language* page to provide some extra support. After students have discussed the three questions, have them share their answers with the class. As a follow-up to question 3, ask the students which quotation they identify with most. Is there another quotation that they agree with more? Are there any work-related quotations in their culture?

Background information

Students may not understand the difference between *work* and *job* because the words are so similar in meaning. Both can refer to what we get paid for doing. However, the words are used in different ways. Collocations come up later in the unit, but you can pave the way to the topic by introducing some expressions with *work (work ethic, hard work, shift work, work experience, go to work, to work your socks off)* and expressions with job *(job satisfaction, job security, find a job, job interview, lose a job, desk job, part-time job, do a good job, temporary job, job opportunities, on-the-job training)*. You could also point out that *work* is a noun and a verb, but *job* is only a noun. *Work* is also a noncount noun, whereas *job* is a count noun.

There is also a pronunciation difficulty with the word *work*, because students from some countries find it difficult to pronounce the difference between *walk* /wɔk/ and *work* /wɜrk/. It may be worth spending some time practicing the difference in pronunciation of these two words.

Vocabulary preview

Students will need to use their dictionaries to look up the new words. Ask them to look up only the words in bold to find similar meanings. Be sure to check students' pronunciation of the words. When they have finished, check the answers with the class.

ANSWERS

1	to reverse	5	downgrade
2	close	6	detailed
3	appearance	7	average
4	annoyed	8	easy

READING 1 The farmer's lazy son

Word count 437

Before you read

Background information

Folktales is a compound word (unit 8)—*folk* = people + *tale* = story. Folktales are traditional stories that are present in every culture. They are often quite simple, but they have a profound message or moral to be learned. They always have themes that are related to humankind and may seek to explain natural events. Because they are traditional, they are oral stories that have been passed down through the generations. Some folktales have trickster characters, such as Anansi in African folktales or Br'er Rabbit in American tales. Folktales are slightly removed from reality—animals can talk, magic is common—and they often involve someone weaker overcoming adversity. You may want to explore the topic of folktales further with your students by getting them to tell a popular folktale from their culture.

To introduce the topic of folktales, you could tell a familiar tale (e.g. "Little Red Riding Hood" or "Jack and the Beanstalk"), or one from your culture. Ask the students what the lesson, or *moral*, of the tale is.

Give them some time to think about a folktale from their culture. Then ask them to discuss the questions with a partner. Be sure to refer them to the phrases in the *Morals* box. As a follow-up, ask a few students to share their folktale and its moral with the class.

Global reading

1 Ask students to read the title and predict what they think the moral might be. Then ask them to read ONLY the first paragraph and predict what will happen in the next paragraph. Ask students to give the evidence they used to make their prediction.

ANSWER

1 Someone will find a way to get Paolo to work.

2 Ask the students to read the rest of the story and do the exercise. When students have finished, ask them to share their ideas with the class.

Close reading

1 Students learned about using transitions to sequence events in unit 9. This section looks at sequencing events, but without using sequencers. This requires a closer reading and understanding of the text, and is also a critical thinking skill. Draw students' attention to the information in the *Sequencing* box. Ask students to do the exercise, then check the answers with the class.

> **ANSWERS**
> a 2 b 4 c 6 d 7 e 9 f 12 g 1 h 8 i 11
> j 3 k 10 l 5

2 This exercise revisits another critical thinking skill: author's purpose (unit 2). When students have finished, check the answers with the class.

> **ANSWERS**
> inform
> entertain

Developing critical thinking

Before the students discuss the questions in groups, draw their attention to the words in the *Academic keywords* box. Question 2 requires students to give evidence from the text to support their opinion. Be sure to encourage them to give reasons to back up their opinion. When the groups have finished, ask them to share their ideas with the class.

Extra research task

Ask students to research elements common to all folktales (search for *characteristics of folktales*).

As an alternative, ask students to research folktales from their culture or from another culture. They could do this by using the Internet, or they could interview people in their family. Ask them to write the characters, the story, and the moral. Go through the stages of planning, writing, sharing, rewriting, and editing so that students create their best possible work. Artistic students may like to illustrate some of the stories. You could then collate all the stories into a book that you then photocopy for the class.

READING 2 Leave it for the robot
Word count 456

Before you read

Background information
Labor-saving robots are not a new idea. Humans have been experimenting with ways to get machines to do human labor for centuries. Leonardo da Vinci even designed a mechanical robot warrior. Robots are becoming more and more sophisticated and are continually the focus of futuristic movies, such as the *Terminator* movies; *I, Robot*; and *WALL-E*. They are being built for a vast array of uses, for example, for use in medicine, surgery, industry, home, espionage, automobiles, and, of course, toys. Actroid F is a Japanese-created robot that is incredibly human-like. It is being tested in hospitals in Japan to see if patients feel comfortable talking to a human-like robot.

Ask students to say what they see in the pictures on page 100—robots, robotic arms, rovers, etc. Ask them to discuss the questions, and have them to refer to the *Jobs* box for help. Afterwards, ask students to brainstorm some of the other jobs that robots currently do.

> **ANSWERS**
> Picture 1: preparing food / cooking
> Picture 2: factory work
> Picture 3: exploring

Global reading

1 Give students about three minutes to skim the text and write what it's about. Then ask them to compare answers.

> **ANSWER**
> The text is about different types of robots and what they can do for us.

2 Ask students to read the sentences in exercise 2 before scanning the text quickly for the answers.

> **ANSWERS**
> 1 millions
> 2 mechanical arm
> 3 explore the surface of the moon and Mars; perform maintenance on oil drilling platforms (also: explore the ocean floors, gather information on geographical changes in volcanoes)
> 4 vacuums

Close reading

Introduce the topic of graphs and charts by charting a quick class survey. Ask students how many have a (toy or other) robot at home. Draw a simple pie chart showing the percentage of those students who have one and those who don't. Ask students what the name of this kind of chart is. Then refer them to the *Reading charts and graphs* box to check and learn more. Afterwards, check students' understanding of the information. Ask: *Why do we use graphs and charts? Which graph shows parts of a whole? Which would you use if you wanted to compare two things? What percentage of people think that salary is the most important factor in a job? What is most important for most people? What is least important? What is the most important writing skill for college instructors? Which is the least important skill for college instructors? Which is the most important skill for high school teachers?* etc. If students are feeling confident, you could have them ask each other some questions about the graphs. Remind students of the language of comparison (unit 6) that will help them talk about the bar graph.

1 Ask students to read the text and look at Figure 1. Then ask them to discuss the questions in groups. Check the answers with the class.

> **ANSWERS**
> 1 Spain
> 2 Japan
> 3 Germany

2 Ask students to do the exercise individually, then check the answers with the class.

> **ANSWERS**
> 1 vaccuum cleaning
> 2 around 60%
> 3 sports partner

Developing critical thinking

Ask students to think about some of the things the article says that robots can do. Ask them to compile a list based on the information in the article. Then ask them to compare it to the list they brainstormed earlier in the *Before you read* section.

1 Ask students to discuss the questions in groups. Give each group some large sheets of paper and ask them to write their ideas. When they have finished, hang the papers around the room. Ask students to move around the room and read each other's ideas.

2 Remind students of the text *The farmer's lazy son*. Ask them if they think there is a connection between this text and *Leave it for the robot*. Then ask them to discuss the questions. An alternative way to do the questions is via a poll—ask students to mingle, asking the two questions and recording who they talked to and what their opinion was. Follow up by collating the opinions of the class on the board. Then ask students to draw a graph or chart to display the results. Talk about the results using comparison language.

This is a good place in the lesson to use the video resource *Work and motivation*. It is located in the Video resources section of the Digibook. Alternatively, remind the students about the video resource so they can do this at home.

Academic keywords

Students have now been exposed to 60 academic keywords. This is quite an achievement, so it might be a good idea to point out to students how many academic keywords they have learned over the course of the term. Ask them to go back through the book and check (✓) all the academic keywords they feel they know and double check (✓✓) all the keywords they feel they know and can use.

Vocabulary skill

Remind students of the collocations from the start of the unit. Point out that there is no grammatical rule about which words go together; some words go together because speakers of the language have decided that that is the custom. Ask students to think of similar examples in their language. You may have to pair up students who speak the same language to help them generate ideas. All languages have collocations, so getting students to think about them in their own language can help them realize that it is not such an unusual thing. Ask them to read the *Using collocations* box to find out more about collocations.

1   Ask students to match 1–4 with a–d and 5–8 with e–h. Then check the answers with the class.

A *firm handshake* is a cultural concept—every culture does not have the same opinion about the importance of a firm handshake. Similarly, the idea of deep pockets is quite idiomatic—*to have deep pockets* means to be wealthy.

ANSWERS
1 b   2 d   3 c   4 a   5 h   6 g   7 e   8 f

2   Invite students to use their dictionaries. If you have access to collocation dictionaries, you could bring them in for students to use. Make sure students understand the meaning of the collocations. Ask them to provide a synonym, definition, or example.

ANSWERS
1 the housework	6 work
2 a decision	7 sorry
3 a promise	8 an apology
4 thanks	9 a break
5 married	10 a favor

Ask students to find one to two more collocations to go with each verb. Make special note of the *make / do* collocations as they are often confused.

3   This exercise requires students to think carefully about the meaning of the collocations. Ask the students to do the exercise individually, then check the answers with the class.

ANSWERS
1 lunch	6 a visit
2 ready	7 a taxi
3 the laundry	8 calm
4 a mistake	9 the answer
5 overseas	10 energy

WRITING Describing your future

Writing skill

The idea of parallel structure may be completely new to students. First, ensure they know the meaning of the word *parallel*. You can illustrate this with two parallel lines drawn on the board. Write an example sentence on the board, e.g. *My robot cooks, cleans, and does my homework*, underlining the words that are parallel. Ask the students why they think the words are parallel. Point out that they are in the same tense. Show students another sentence in which the words are not parallel: *My robot cooks, cleans, and will do my homework*. Ask students why they think this sentence is NOT parallel. Ask them to read the *Using parallel structure* box. Then ask questions to check their comprehension. Ask: *What tense are the verbs in the first sentence? Why did the writer not say, I'll take … I'll go … I'll swim …?* (*I'll* is understood and so it can be omitted.) Ask students to underline or highlight the words in the sentences without parallel structure: *I'll take / go / swimming; staying / sleeping / spent.* Correct the incorrect sentences together.

1   Ask students to work individually to do the exercise, then check the answers with the class.

ANSWERS
1   In 1939, a robot named Elektro was able to <u>walk</u>, <u>count</u> on its fingers, and <u>spoke</u> words.
2   Most robots today are used to doing jobs that are <u>repetitive</u>, <u>mundane</u>, or <u>danger</u>.
3   Robots are also used in factories to build things like <u>cars</u>, <u>appliances</u>, and <u>make electronics</u>.
4   Some robots are designed to <u>explore</u> underwater, <u>go</u> down into volcanoes, and <u>traveling</u> to other planets.
5   Robots have been sent to Mars to <u>collect</u> soil, rock and atmosphere samples, <u>analyze</u> them, and then <u>will send</u> the data back to Earth.
6   Another reason we use robots is because they never <u>get</u> sick, <u>take</u> a day off, or <u>complained</u>!
7   Most robots usually have at least three main parts— the "brain" <u>that is run by a computer program</u>, mechanical parts <u>that make the robot move</u>, and sensors <u>to tell the robot about its surroundings</u>.
8   Unlike in TV programs, robots are unable to <u>think</u>, <u>feel</u>, or <u>makes</u> decisions.

2   Check to make sure the students have the correct answers to exercise 1 before moving on to the next exercise. When the students have finished, check the answers with the class.

ANSWERS

1 In 1939, a robot named *Elektro* was able to walk, count on its fingers, and speak words.
2 Most robots today are used to doing jobs that are repetitive, mundane, or dangerous.
3 Robots are also used in factories to build things like cars, appliances, and electronics.
4 Some robots are designed to explore underwater, go down into volcanoes, and travel to other planets.
5 Robots have been sent to Mars to collect soil, rock, and atmosphere samples, analyze them, and then send the data back to Earth.
6 Another reason we use robots is because they never get sick, take a day off, or complain!
7 Most robots usually have at least three main parts—the "brain" that is run by a computer program, mechanical parts that make the robot move, and sensors that tell the robot about its surroundings.
8 Unlike in TV programs, robots are unable to think, feel, or make decisions.

Grammar

Background information

The simple future tense is not a difficult one for most students to grasp, though students can make mistakes in the situations in which they use it, so be sure to draw students' attention to the four situations in which *will* is used. If students want to know when to use other future forms, it might be a good time to review the other tenses which are used for the future, making sure to highlight the situations that call for the tense: present simple for timetables (*The plane leaves at 3 p.m.*); present continuous for future arrangements (*I'm playing tennis with him tomorrow.*).

Many students have a problem hearing the "dark L" sound in the contracted forms—*I'll, you'll, she'll*, etc. This /l/ sound is different to the one in *love* or *lost*; it is pronounced further back in the throat, which is why it is called the "dark L." Ask students to repeat as you drill the contracted forms. Explain that the contracted forms are used in spoken English while the full forms are used in formal writing. Once students have practiced pronouncing the contracted forms, do a little listening exercise in which you contrast the forms. Ask students to write what they hear as you dictate the sentences at normal speed (not slowed down): *He'll go tomorrow. She helps her friend*, etc. Tell students they can use grammatical clues to get the sentence right even if they can't quite hear the "dark L."

You may also want to contrast the difference in pronunciation between *won't* /wəʊnt/ and *want* /wɑnt/. Repeat the procedure above for these contrasting, yet easily confused, words. Again, grammatical clues will help students decide which was said.

1 After students have read the *Grammar* box, ask them to close their book and tell you four situations in which the simple future tense is used. Give some other examples of the four situations. You may need to explain *spontaneous decision* in more depth. To help students connect the situation with the tense more clearly, try to think of people to connect the situations to. For example, to express a promise—a politician, to make a prediction—a fortune-teller or a weather person, etc. Ask students to do the exercise, then check the answers with the class.

ANSWERS

1 d   2 a   3 c   4 b

2 Ask the students to work individually to complete the sentences, then check the answers with the class. If going over the answers orally, check that students are pronouncing the contracted form correctly.

ANSWERS

1 will finish	4 will quit
2 will work	5 will look
3 will not / won't rain	6 will do

3 Ask students to work individually to write predictions, then compare their ideas with a partner.

EXTENSION ACTIVITY

You could hold a mock election. Ask students to imagine they are running for president. What will they promise the people in order to get elected? Ask them to write down a few ideas, then put them into groups of three. Ask one person to give his/her "election promises" to the other two, e.g. *If you elect me, I will* … Repeat with the other two students. Ask each group to "vote" on who made the best election promises.

WRITING TASK

Ask students what they think a *bright future* might be. Is it positive or negative? Ask them to read the model paragraph and follow the instructions. When they have finished, check the answers with the class.

I think that my future <u>will be</u> very bright. I'm currently in my third year of college and next year I <u>will be</u> a senior. After I graduate, I <u>will</u> probably <u>travel</u> for a couple of weeks, see some friends, and then to look for a job. I'm studying to be an engineer so I would like to get a job in an engineering firm in my hometown. It <u>won't be</u> easy, but I <u>will do</u> my best. In three years I think I <u>will try</u> to buy a house. I want a house that is near my parents, that isn't too expensive, and that isn't far from work. I don't know, but I hope I <u>will be</u> married in four years. I'd like to start a family in about five years. I'm sure I <u>will have</u> a lot of children someday. That's what I think <u>will happen</u>, but of course no one can predict the future!

Brainstorm, plan, and write

Ask students to think individually for a few moments, and then brainstorm their future with a partner in order to generate more ideas. Then ask them to complete the timeline with some of their ideas.

Tell students to use as many ideas from their timeline as possible. They may want to highlight some of the things that they can group together in order to use parallel structure.

When students have finished planning, ask them to write about 150 words for their paragraph.

Share, rewrite, and edit

Ask students to exchange their paragraphs with a partner. Encourage students to use the Peer review checklist on page 109 when they are evaluating their partner's paragraph.

Ask students to rewrite and edit their paragraphs. Encourage them to take into consideration their partner's feedback when rewriting.

Use the photocopiable unit assignment checklist on page 97 to assess the students' paragraphs.

To finish off, why not have a team vocabulary game? Tell each team to draw a circle in the center of a piece of paper. Then ask them to write the word you give them in the circle (choose a unit topic, e.g. *character, time, home,* etc.). Set a timer for three minutes. The teams must make a word map with all the words and expressions they can think of that go with the topic. At the end of the three minutes, ask each team to count how many words they wrote. The winning team is the one with the most correct words. Repeat as many times as you think you can keep students engaged (three or four more times, probably).

STUDY SKILLS Making the most of the library

Background information

Recently, a new university student proudly announced that he had never set foot in a library. He then spent the rest of the semester trying to maintain his record. Unfortunately, many students could share the same boast. With the Internet offering so much information, the effort of getting to a library and learning how to use it can seem outdated and pointless.

However, the library still has value and much to offer. There students can find scholarly materials that are more suitable for study than many Internet resources. Resources are also grouped so that it is easy to find materials related to a single topic. Plus, the resources are free. There are study sections that provide a quiet atmosphere in which to study and group areas where students can study together. And importantly, there is always someone there to help students find what they need.

Many libraries now have their catalogues online so that they can be accessed from home. This is a useful tool for finding out if the library has a particular resource. Often, if not, an order can be placed via the site for an interlibrary loan. Usually the library then alerts you via email when the book is available to pick up.

If possible, take your students to the school or local library. There may be someone there who can give a tour. If not, divide the students into groups and ask them to find out the answers to the questions in the *Find out basic information* box. It would also be a good time for students to apply for a library card—check to find out what information or identification they need to bring with them when applying for a library card.

Start by giving students one minute to brainstorm all the services and resources that the library offers. Collate their ideas on the board afterwards, then direct students to the list of services in the *Library services* section for comparison. Make sure students understand what the terms mean and why the services are useful.

Ask students to read the *Make the library our own* section, and discuss what they already know about their local or school library. You could use this as an opportunity to state some basic library rules: try to be as quiet as possible, don't put books back on the shelves—leave them on the tables or racks, anyone can use the computers and tables, etc. If it is not possible to arrange a group trip to the library, ask students to go on their own for homework. Ask them to find out the answers to the questions in the *Find out basic information* box. Encourage them to ask the librarian—that's what they are there for!

Useful language

✂

brave /breɪv/	caring /kerɪŋ/
clever /ˈklevər/	confident /ˈkɑnfədənt/
funny /ˈfʌni/	helpful /ˈhelpfəl/
lazy /ˈleɪzi/	loud /laʊd/
outgoing /aʊtˈgoʊɪŋ/	quiet /ˈkwaɪət/
reliable /rɪˈlaɪəbəl/	selfish /ˈselfɪʃ/

✂

accurate /'ækjərət/	alarm clock /ə'lɑrm klɑk/
clock /klɑk/	cog /kɑg/
hands /hændz/	hours /aʊrz/
metal /'met(ə)l/	minutes /'mɪnɪts/
set /set/	time /taɪm/
wake up /weɪk ʌp/	watch /watʃ/

Useful language

airy
/ˈeəri/

comfortable
/ˈkʌmfərtəbəl/

cozy
/ˈkoʊzi/

cramped
/kræmpt/

dark
/dɑrk/

light
/laɪt/

luxurious
/ləgˈʒʊriəs/

modern
/ˈmɑdərn/

old-fashioned
/ˈoʊldˈfæʃənd/

simple
/ˈsɪmpəl/

spacious
/ˈspeɪʃəs/

uncomfortable
/ʌnˈkʌmfərtəbəl/

Skillful Level 1 Reading & Writing Teacher's Book.
This page is photocopiable, but all copies must be complete pages.
© Macmillan Publishers Limited 2013.

ant /ænt/	bird /bɜrd/
elephant /ˈeləfənt/	enormous /ɪˈnɔrməs/
flea /fli/	giraffe /dʒəˈræf/
huge /hjudʒ/	mouse /maʊs/
rhinoceros /raɪˈnasərəs/	shrimp /ʃrɪmp/
tiny /ˈtaɪni/	whale /weɪl/

UNIT 5

Useful language

black-and-white
/ˈblækənˈhwaɪt/

circular
/ˈsɜrkjələr/

colorful
/ˈkʌlərfəl/

curved line
/kɜrvd laɪn/

flowery
/ˈflaʊəri/

irregular
/ɪˈregjələr/

patterned
/ˈpætərnd/

plain
/pleɪn/

regular
/ˈregjələr/

spotted
/spatɪd/

straight line
/streɪt laɪn/

striped
/straɪpt/

wavy
/ˈweɪvi/

chat
/tʃæt/

cook
/kʊk/

cycle
/ˈsaɪkəl/

drink tea or coffee
/drɪŋk ti ɔrˈkɔfi/

drive
/draɪv/

eat meals
/it milz/

exercise
/ˈeksərˌsaɪz/

run
/rʌn/

shop
/ʃap/

walk
/wɔk/

work
/wɜrk/

✂

black /blæk/	blue /blu/
brown /braʊn/	dark /dɑrk/
green /grin/	light /laɪt/
orange /ˈɔrɪndʒ/	pink /pɪŋk/
purple /ˈpɜrpəl/	red /red/
white /waɪt/	yellow /ˈjeloʊ/

Africa
/ˈæfrɪkə/

Antarctica
/ænˈtɑːktɪkə/

Asia
/ˈeɪʒə/

Australasia
/ˌɒstrəˈleɪʒə/

continent
/ˈkɒntənənt/

east
/iːst/

Europe
/ˈjʊərəp/

north
/nɔːθ/

North America
/nɔːθ əˈmerɪkə/

south
/saʊθ/

South America
/saʊθ əˈmerɪkə/

west
/west/

education
/ˌedʒəˈkeɪʃən/

fame
/feɪm/

family
/ˈfæməli/

friendship
/ˈfrendʃɪp/

happiness
/ˈhæpinəs/

home
/hoʊm/

love
/lʌv/

money
/ˈmʌni/

religion
/rɪˈlɪdʒən/

success
/səkˈses/

travel
/ˈtrævəl/

work
/wɜrk/

Skillful Level 1 Reading & Writing Teacher's Book.
This page is photocopiable, but all copies must be complete pages.
© Macmillan Publishers Limited 2013.

backbreaking /ˈbækˌbreɪkɪŋ/	beneficial /ˌbenəˈfɪʃəl/
boring /ˈbɔrɪŋ/	dangerous /ˈdeɪndʒərəs/
dirty /ˈdɜrti/	educational /ˌedʒəˈkeɪʃənəl/
fun /fʌn	hard /hard/
interesting /ˈɪntrəstɪŋ/	rewarding /rɪˈwɔrdɪŋ/
satisfying /ˈsætəsˌfaɪɪŋ/	tedious /ˈtidiəs/

Unit assignment

UNIT 1 CHARACTER

Student name: _____

Date: _____

Unit assignment: Everyday heroes

25 points: Excellent achievement. Student successfully fulfils the expectation for this part of the assignment with little or no room for improvement.

20 points: Good achievement. Student fulfils the expectation for this part of the assignment, but may have a few errors or need some improvement.

15 points: Satisfactory achievement. Student needs some work to fulfil the expectation for this part of the assignment, but shows some effort.

5 points: Poor achievement. Student does not fulfil the expectation for this part of the assignment.

	Met		Unmet		Comments
The paragraph is 100–120 words in length.					
	25 points	20 points	15 points	5 points	
The paragraph has a topic sentence which introduces the main idea.					
The sentences in the paragraph support the main idea of the topic sentence.					
The paragraph uses the simple present tense correctly.					
The paragraph uses appropriate vocabulary.					

Total: _____ /100

Comments:

UNIT 2 TIME

Student name: _____

Date: _____

Unit assignment: How to achieve my goal

25 points: Excellent achievement. Student successfully fullfils the expectation for this part of the assignment with little or no room for improvement

20 points: Good achievement. Student fulfills the expectation for this part of the assignment, but may have a few errors or need some improvement.

15 points: Satisfactory achievement. Student needs some work to fulfill the expectation for this part of the assignment, but shows some effort.

5 points: Poor achievement. Student does not fulfill the expectation for this part of the assignment.

	Met		Unmet		Comments
The paragraph is 100–150 words in length.					
	25 points	20 points	15 points	5 points	
The paragraph has a topic sentence that introduces the goal.					
The writer has said why he/she would like to achieve the goal and has listed three things that he/she can do to achieve the goal.					
The paragraph uses a variety of sentence patterns, including gerunds and infinitives.					
The paragraph uses appropriate vocabulary.					

Total points: _____ /100

Comments:

Unit assignment

Student name: _____

Date: _____

Unit assignment: My home

25 points: Excellent achievement. Student successfully fulfils the expectation for this part of the assignment with little or no room for improvement.

20 points: Good achievement. Student fulfils the expectation for this part of the assignment, but may have a few errors or need some improvement.

15 points: Satisfactory achievement. Student needs some work to fulfil the expectation for this part of the assignment, but shows some effort.

5 points: Poor achievement. Student does not fulfil the expectation for this part of the assignment.

	Met		Unmet		Comments
The paragraph is 100–150 words in length.					
	25 points	20 points	15 points	5 points	
The paragraph has a topic sentence that introduces the goal.					
The paragraph has a lot of detail about the home organized into themes.					
The paragraph uses *there is / there are* and quantifiers correctly.					
The paragraph uses appropriate vocabulary.					

Total: _____ /100

Comments:

UNIT 4 SIZE

Student name: _____

Date: _____

Unit assignment: How my neighborhood is changing

25 points: Excellent achievement. Student successfully fulfils the expectation for this part of the assignment with little or no room for improvement.

20 points: Good achievement. Student fulfils the expectation for this part of the assignment, but may have a few errors or need some improvement.

15 points: Satisfactory achievement. Student needs some work to fulfil the expectation for this part of the assignment, but shows some effort.

5 points: Poor achievement. Student does not fulfil the expectation for this part of the assignment.

	Met		Unmet		Comments
The paragraph is 100–150 words in length.					
	25 points	20 points	15 points	5 points	
The paragraph has a topic sentence that introduces the main idea.					
Some of the sentences are linked with *and*, *but*, *or*, and *so*.					
The paragraph uses the present progressive tense correctly.					
The paragraph uses appropriate vocabulary.					

Total: _____ /100

Comments:

Unit assignment

Student name: _____

Date: _____

Unit assignment: Email giving advice

25 points: Excellent achievement. Student successfully fulfills the expectation for this part of the assignment with little or no room for improvement.

20 points: Good achievement. Student fulfills the expectation for this part of the assignment, but may have a few errors or need some improvement.

15 points: Satisfactory achievement. Student needs some work to fulfill the expectation for this part of the assignment, but shows some effort.

5 points: Poor achievement. Student does not fulfill the expectation for this part of the assignment.

	Met		Unmet		Comments
The paragraph is 100–150 words in length.					
	25 points	20 points	15 points	5 points	
The paragraph has a topic sentence that introduces the main idea.					
The paragraph uses correct punctuation and capitalization.					
The paragraph uses *should / should not* and other expressions for giving advice and suggestions.					
The paragraph uses appropriate vocabulary.					

Total: _____ /100

Comments:

UNIT 6 SPEED

Student name: _____

Date: _____

Unit assignment: A comparison

25 points: Excellent achievement. Student successfully fulfils the expectation for this part of the assignment with little or no room for improvement.

20 points: Good achievement. Student fulfils the expectation for this part of the assignment, but may have a few errors or need some improvement.

15 points: Satisfactory achievement. Student needs some work to fulfil the expectation for this part of the assignment, but shows some effort.

5 points: Poor achievement. Student does not fulfil the expectation for this part of the assignment.

	Met		Unmet		Comments
The paragraph is 100–150 words in length.					
	25 points	20 points	15 points	5 points	
The paragraph has a topic sentence that introduces the main idea.					
The paragraph uses correct punctuation (commas and colons) and capitalization.					
The paragraph uses correct comparative forms of adjectives and adverbs.					
The paragraph uses appropriate vocabulary.					

Total: _____ /100

Comments:

Student name: _____

Date: _____

Unit assignment: Colors and their symbolism

25 points: Excellent achievement. Student successfully fulfills the expectation for this part of the assignment with little or no room for improvement.

20 points: Good achievement. Student fulfills the expectation for this part of the assignment, but with occasional errors and hesitancy.

15 points: Satisfactory achievement. Student needs some work to fulfill the expectation for this part of the assignment, but shows some effort.

5 points: Poor achievement. Student does not fulfill the expectation for this part of the assignment.

	Met		Unmet		Comments
The paragraph is 100–150 words in length.					
	25 points	20 points	15 points	5 points	
The paragraph has a topic sentence that introduces the main idea.					
The paragraph contains sentences and does not contain fragments.					
The paragraph uses count and nouncount nouns correctly.					
The paragraph uses appropriate vocabulary.					

Total: _____ /100

Comments:

UNIT 8 EXTREMES

Student name: _____

Date: _____

Unit assignment: Sports

25 points: Excellent achievement. Student successfully fulfils the expectation for this part of the assignment with little or no room for improvement.

20 points: Good achievement. Student fulfils the expectation for this part of the assignment, but may have a few errors or need some improvement.

15 points: Satisfactory achievement. Student needs some work to fulfil the expectation for this part of the assignment, but shows some effort.

5 points: Poor achievement. Student does not fulfil the expectation for this part of the assignment.

	Met		Unmet		Comments
The paragraph is 100–150 words in length.					
	25 points	20 points	15 points	5 points	
The paragraph has a topic sentence which introduces the main idea.					
The paragraph uses transitions correctly to add and emphasize information.					
The paragraph uses appropriate ways of expressing ability.					
The paragraph uses appropriate vocabulary.					

Total: _____ /100

Comments:

UNIT 9 LIFE

Student name: _____

Date: _____

Unit assignment: A memorable day

25 points: Excellent achievement. Student successfully fulfils the expectation for this part of the assignment with little or no room for improvement.

20 points: Good achievement. Student fulfils the expectation for this part of the assignment, but may have a few errors or need some improvement.

15 points: Satisfactory achievement. Student needs some work to fulfil the expectation for this part of the assignment, but shows some effort.

5 points: Poor achievement. Student does not fulfil the expectation for this part of the assignment.

	Met		Unmet		Comments
The paragraph is 100–150 words in length.					
	25 points	20 points	15 points	5 points	
The paragraph has a topic sentence that introduces the main idea.					
The paragraph has a variety of transitions to sequence events in the paragraph.					
The paragraph uses the past tense correctly.					
The paragraph uses appropriate vocabulary.					

Total: _____ /100

Comments:

UNIT 10 WORK

Student name: _____

Date: _____

Unit assignment: My future

25 points: Excellent achievement. Student successfully fulfils the expectation for this part of the assignment with little or no room for improvement.

20 points: Good achievement. Student fulfils the expectation for this part of the assignment, but may have a few errors or need some improvement.

15 points: Satisfactory achievement. Student needs some work to fulfil the expectation for this part of the assignment, but shows some effort.

5 points: Poor achievement. Student does not fulfil the expectation for this part of the assignment.

	Met		Unmet		Comments
The paragraph is 100–150 words in length.					
	25 points	20 points	15 points	5 points	
The paragraph has a topic sentence that introduces the main idea.					
There are at least two examples of parallel structure in the paragraph.					
The paragraph uses the simple future tense correctly.					
The paragraph uses appropriate vocabulary and collocations.					

Total: _____ /100

Comments:

UNIT 1 Character

Vocabulary preview

1 d	4 b	7 f	10 i
2 e	5 c	8 g	
3 a	6 j	9 h	

READING 1 Are you a natural leader?

Before you read

1

Possible answer:

All possess leadership qualities such as intelligence and confidence.

Global reading

It is a survey or questionnaire you would find in a magazine. You would complete the survey to find out if you were a natural leader.

Close reading

2

a 12 b 17 c 1 d 8 e 14 f 18

3

a 20 b 2 c 7 d 9 e 11 f 13

READING 2 The hero within

Before you read

2

The article is about what makes a superhero.

Global reading

1 super-human powers	5 super-villain
2 secret identity	6 backstory
3 colorful costume	7 weakness
4 strong moral code	

Close reading

1

Possible answers:

1 rebirth	5 uninteresting
2 identity	6 human nature
3 strong moral code	7 crime and war
4 good and evil	8 perfect

2

1

a all superheroes   b the law

2

a a weakness   b a superhero

3

a our own fears

b our own fears

Vocabulary skill

1

1 b 2 b 3 a

2

1 a 2 b 3 b

WRITING Describing a hero

Writing skill

1

1 T 2 F 3 T 4 F 5 F

2

Paragraph 1: What makes a superhero, and why are they likely not going anywhere soon?

Paragraph 2: Nearly all fictional superheroes have super-human powers.

Paragraph 3: A secret identity helps protect the superhero's family and friends.

Paragraph 4: A colorful costume, such as Spider-Man's web design or Captain America's U.S. flag costume, helps the public recognize the superhero, and at the same time it hides his or her identity.

Paragraph 5: All superheroes are honest and possess a strong moral code.

Paragraph 6: Superheroes would not exist without the super-villain.

Paragraph 7: The backstory tells how the superhero actually became the superhero we know.

Paragraph 8: A weakness can make a superhero helpless.

Paragraph 9: The superhero is perhaps not so different from us.

3

1 b 2 b 3 b

4

Possible answers:

1

Superhero movies can teach us about ourselves. Superhero movies are not just for children.

2

I possess both positive and negative qualities. My personality has changed over time.

3

There are everyday heroes all around us. Teachers are the true everyday heroes in our lives.

Grammar

1

1 think	3 like	5 see
2 has	4 know	6 belong

2

1 I do not think superhero stories are just for kids.

2 My brother does not have a lot of comic books.

3 My friends and I do not like the X-Men.

4 I do not know the plots of most superhero stories.

5 Our teacher does not see hero qualities in us.

6 These comic books do not belong to my cousin.

WRITING TASK

Everyone has a hero. I think that everyday heroes like police officers and firefighters are true heroes. My hero is my Uncle Manuel. He works as a police officer. I really respect him. He protects our city and keeps us safe. He works long and difficult hours. For example, he often works from 11:00 p.m. to 7:00 a.m. He has to cope with a stressful and difficult job, but he never complains. He is a very honest man. He does not make much money. He does this work because he cares about people. He wants to help them and contribute something to our city. People sometimes thank him. I want more people to do that. We need to appreciate these everyday heroes more.

STUDY SKILLS Setting up a study space

Scenario

Possible answer:

Hamid has a large workspace and can spread out his books. However, he shouldn't lie on his bed to work or have the TV on. He should ask his brother not to come in when he is studying.

UNIT 2 Time

Vocabulary preview

1 a 2 a 3 b 4 a 5 a 6 a 7 b

READING 1 A matter of time

Before you read

2

1 It's about time management.

2 It shows the expression "time flies." In other words, it shows that time passes quickly.

Global reading

1 Write it down

2 Prioritize

3 Don't skip the breaks

4 One thing at a time

5 Schedule email time

6 Choose to say "no"

7 Keep a goal journal

Close reading

1

a 5 b 3 c 4 d 6 e 1 f 7 g 2

2

1 inform

READING 2 What time is it?

Global reading

2 A history of clocks

Close reading

1

1 c 2 e 3 a 4 d 5 b 6 f

2

1 It was smaller.

2 It was impossible to tell time on cloudy days or at night.

3 They were used in Egypt, the Middle East, and China.

4 Clocks began to be more accurate in the thirteenth century.

5 Springs improved their accuracy.

6 People started to rely on clocks to run businesses after 1927, when the quartz clock was invented.

Vocabulary skill

1

1 N	3 V	5 N	7 N
2 V	4 N	6 N	8 V

2

1 Are you wearing a watch?

2 Many years ago there were no clocks.

3 Its shadow marked the movement of the sun.

4 They were able to determine midday.

5 After midday they had to move it 180 degrees.

6 At night it was impossible to tell time.

7 These clocks were popular in the Middle East.

8 Over the next few centuries the design was developed.

3

Nouns: blogs, post, information, stress, life, time, advice, breaks, idea

Verbs: read, enjoyed, was, have, know, manage, was, want, thank

WRITING Describing how to achieve a goal

Writing skill

1

1 S + V	4 S + V + IO + DO
2 S + V + DO	5 S + V
3 S + V + DO	6 S + V + IO + DO

2

1 Kevin plans to skip class.
  (S + V + DO)

2 Sachiko refused to text. (S + V)

3 Lucas relies on his cell phone.
  (S + V + DO)

4 Omar has sent me five emails.
  (S + V + IO + DO)

Grammar

1

1 to understand; working

2 to miss, skipping

3 to speak

4 writing

5 to keep / keeping

6 studying

2

1 to take	4 to continue
2 to reduce	5 getting
3 to do	6 to think / thinking

WRITING TASK

I like going for bike rides, and I love going for long walks. Unfortunately, I don't seem to have time for these things anymore. I'd like to have more free time for myself so I can do the things I enjoy doing. To achieve this, I will do several things. I plan to write down my appointments and then I will prioritize them. I hate to forget things, and this sometimes happens. I'll be more organized this way. I have a part-time job and I hope to reduce my hours from 15 to 12 hours per week. I also need to say "no" to my friends more. They often rely on me for homework help and I have to avoid saying "yes" every time. I want to be more honest and straightforward with them about my time commitments. If I achieve these things, I'll be able to have more free time.

UNIT 3 Home

Vocabulary preview

1 location	5 resources
2 distinctive	6 lifestyle
3 typical	7 traditions
4 routine	8 unique

READING 1 Home is where the heart is

Before you read

Possible answers:

"There is no place like home."

One's home is the best place of all.

"Love makes a house a home."

A home is more than the building. It's a place of love and family.

"Home follows the family."

If you move to a new place, it is the family that makes it a home.

"Home is where the heart is."

If you are with the person or place you love the most, it becomes your true home.

Global reading

Paragraph 1: a	Paragraph 4: a
Paragraph 2: b	Paragraph 5: b
Paragraph 3: a	

Close reading

2

1 T	3 F	5 T	7 NG
2 NG	4 T	6 F	8 T

READING 2 Home automation

Global reading

2 The smartest home in the world

Close reading

1

Possible answers:

turns on lights

waters the yard

adjusts the thermostat

opens the curtains

answers the phone

calls his children for dinner

wakes him up

opens his bedroom curtains

starts his shower and sets the temperature

turns on the TV news

turns up the air conditioning

monitors local weather

informs him about traffic conditions

keeps him updated on his favorite sports teams and scores

monitors online activity

suspends operation of their computers and TVs

Vocabulary skill

1

Possible answers:

1 make changes

2 do something when you are far away from it

3 shuts down

2

1 area   2 work with   3 develop

WRITING Describing your home

Grammar

1

1 is   2 are   3 are   4 is   5 is   6 are

7 is   8 are

2

1 one	5 a
2 much	6 some
3 few	7 a
4 great deal of	8 many

WRITING TASK

I live in an apartment building. It's about 30 minutes from the city center. There are a lot of similar apartment buildings around mine. There are a few small stores near us but there aren't any nice restaurants or cafes. My building is 18 stories high and I live on the seventh floor. There are five main rooms in the apartment. When you enter, there is a large living room. The kitchen is next to it. There are two bedrooms – one for my parents and one for my little sister and me. I like the apartment a lot, although it is small. There is only one bathroom and there are not many closets. Someday I'd like to have a bigger home with more closets.

STUDY SKILLS Reviewing and practicing vocabulary

Scenario

Possible answer:

Lucy works hard and uses definitions, examples, and pictures. However, she should review the words more and try categorizing them.

UNIT 4 Size

Vocabulary preview

1

1 e	4 b	7 h
2 d	5 c	8 i
3 a	6 g	9 f

2

1 abundant	6 primary
2 demand	7 approximately
3 population	8 efficient
4 massive	9 concentration
5 Aside from	

READING 1 Fuel of the sea

Global reading

2 Krill are a primary food source for many sea animals.

Close reading

1

Blue whales eat krill.

Blues whales eat about four tons of food each day.

Some penguin populations are decreasing in number because there are fewer krill, their food source.

2

1 Krill are tiny, shrimp-like animals.

2 They live in all the world's oceans.

3 Whales, fish, seals, and penguins eat krill.

4 Krill swarms can get as large as 450 square kilometers.

5 Loss of sea ice, demand for krill oil, and fishing are causing krill numbers to decline.

6 Some animals that feed on krill, such as penguins, have declined in number.

READING 2 Size doesn't matter

Before you read

1

The country is Singapore.

It is in Asia.

English is the most widely spoken language.

Global reading

2

How Singapore became successful even with little land.

Close reading

1

1 15.5 **2** 7,300 **3** 24,000 **4** 100 **5** 3

2

Statements you can infer: 1, 2, 3, 4, 5

Vocabulary skill

1

1 tiny shrimp-like animals

2 single-cell plants at the bottom of the food chain

3 fish, seals, and penguins

4 swarm

2

1 a small country at the tip of the Malay Peninsula

2 an island resort at the southern end of the country

3 Indian, Chinese, and Malay influences

4 a large, smelly, and spiky fruit

5 one of the Asian "tigers"

3

1 large

2 about or not exactly

3 plentiful

4 *Demand*

5 *population*

WRITING Describing how your neighborhood is changing

Writing skill

1

1 and   **4** so   **7** but   **10** so

2 so   **5** and   **8** or

3 or   **6** so   **9** but

2

1 The signs in Singapore are in English, so it is easy to get around.

2 There is a park in my neighborhood, but no one goes there.

3 You can easily get a taxi on the street, or it is easy to call for a taxi.

4 I have a lot of friends in my neighborhood and they all live nearby.

Grammar

1

1 is changing   **5** am paying

2 are buying   **6** is making

3 are investing   **7** are starting

4 is pushing   **8** are shopping

2

1

a are closing   **b** know

2

a are beginning   **b** wants

3

a is taking   **b** needs

4

a are planning   **b** Are you saving

WRITING TASK

My neighborhood is changing a lot. Some of these are positive changes, but some are negative. More people are moving into the neighborhood. This is a positive thing. These new residents are shopping in the neighborhood, so they are spending money locally. This helps local businesses a lot, and develops a sense of community. A lot of new buildings are going up as well, but I don't think this is a good thing. It is creating a lot of noise, and many of the new homes are sitting empty. There are now a lot of new homes, but there are some older, empty homes. There are more children in the neighborhood now, but no one is building more parks, and I know we will need more of these in the future. Overall, I think the way the neighborhood is changing is a positive thing.

STUDY SKILLS Process writing

Scenario

Possible answer:

Chen wrote his assignment in a quiet study space, and had his friend give him feedback. However, he should have edited his paper carefully for spelling, punctuation, and grammar errors before he handed it in.

Consider it

Chen did steps: pre-writing, writing, sharing, revising, submission.

UNIT 5 Patterns

Vocabulary preview

1 b **2** c **3** a **4** d **5** g **6** e **7** f

READING 1 Time for a change

Before you read

The picture shows a man running because he is late

Global reading

2 Ideas for breaking bad habits.

Close reading

1

1

a M **b** S

2

a M **b** S

3

a M **b** S

4

a M **b** S

5

a M **b** S

2

1 d **2** e **3** a **4** c **5** b

READING 2 The Fibonacci sequence

Before you read

Possible answer:

They all have an attractive, circular pattern.

Global reading

2 Nature's numbering system

Close reading

3

1 F **2** F **3** F **4** T **5** F

Vocabulary skill

1

1 unrealistic   **7** irresponsible

2 dissatisfied   **8** inconsiderate

3 unpopular   **9** impersonal

4 irrational   **10** unbelievable

5 inefficient   **11** illegal

6 impolite   **12** disrespectful

2

1 I am disorganized.

2 It is impossible.

3 It is illegal.

4 It is irregular.

5 It is unrealistic.

6 Your answer is incorrect.

7 It is illogical.

8 It is unlikely.

WRITING Giving advice in an email

Writing skill

1

Possible answers:

1

a Guess what! I solved this math problem – finally! I hope it's correct.

b Congratulations! I know math isn't your favorite subject.

2

a Did you hear about Maggie? She cut up all her credit cards!

b She did? I knew she wanted to change some of her shopping habits.

3

a Quick! Look over there!

b That's amazing! But what, exactly, is it?

2

1 The Fibonacci numbers can be seen in the Taj Mahal in India.

2 Please ask Mother and Father what time dinner is.

3 Today is Tuesday, April 13.

4 Is the test on a Monday or Tuesday?

5 My favorite book is *Of Mice and Men*.

6 Venezuela is a country in the northern part of South America.

7 Omar speaks English, Arabic, and French.

8 Drive west until you get to the town of East Dayton.

9 Mr. and Mrs. Peterson moved to New York City last summer.

10 The Red Sea separates East Africa from the Arabian Peninsula.

Grammar

1

1 It is good to make shopping lists.
2 You should buy things on sale.
3 You should not eat out so much.
4 It is important to take public transportation.
5 You have to open a savings account.
6 You need to keep a budget.
7 You should be careful with your credit cards.
8 It is not good to buy designer goods.

2

1 You needs to address the person first.
2 You should to include a clear subject line.
3 It is a good to keep things short and simple.
4 It is important to remember that emails are permanent.
5 It is ideal to should answer emails right away.
6 You should not wrote write things you would not say.
7 You should checking the email before you send it.
8 It's not good to type in capital letters.

WRITING TASK

To: Terry@email.com
Subject: my advice
Hi Terry,
I got your email last Saturday asking me for my advice about studying in London. First, congratulations! I'm happy you got accepted. My summer program there was great. Are you also planning to start the program in July? There are some excellent professors there. You should write to Professor Radison. She can help answer some questions, too. I will send you her email. They have a booklet for new students called "Tips for New Students" and I'm sure she will send you that.
It's good to arrive early so you can get settled before classes start. It's important to reserve an early place if you want to live in the dorms. You need to apply for a place before March. You shouldn't worry, though. I think there is plenty of time. Or are you going to rent an apartment? I'm really glad I can help. Write me back with specific questions.
Robin

UNIT 6 Speed

Vocabulary preview

1 appeal
2 impact
3 pace
4 associate
5 origin
6 emphasized
7 advocate
8 functional

READING 1 Hurry up and slow down!

Global reading

1 Who the movement attracts
2 How the movement started
4 How the movement's ideas spread

Close reading

1

1 inform

2

1 O 2 O 3 F 4 O 5 O

READING 2 Keeping up with the Tarahumara

Global reading

2 The tradition of long-distance running among the Tarahumara

Close reading

1

2 admiring

2

Possible answer:

runs effortlessly, remarkably, such good runners, incredibly, famous in the running world, admired as world-class athletes

3

1 They live in the canyon country of northern Mexico.
2 It means "foot runner."
3 A pueblo is bigger than a rancho.
4 They grow corn and beans.
5 Their running courses may be anywhere between 48 and 160 kilometers long.
6 Victoriano got first place.

4

Statements you can infer: 1, 2, 4, 5, 6

Vocabulary skill

1

1 ADV   4 ADJ   7 ADJ
2 ADJ   5 ADV   8 ADJ
3 ADV   6 ADJ

2

1 sometimes
2 now
3 careful
4 slow
5 comfortable
6 there
7 famous
8 quickly

WRITING Making a comparison

Writing skill

1

1 You will need to bring three things: a notebook, pens, and a calculator.
2 A lot of people like to travel at high speeds, but I hate it.
3 Like many people, I have an online profile.
4 She works all day. In addition, she takes classes at night.
5 If I can give you one piece of advice it is this: exercise.
6 Before you start running, it is good to do a 15-minutes warm-up.
7 I love to run, but my friends hate to run.
8 My father always says, "Slow down! No one is going to take your food away."

2

Since its formation, the Slow Food Movement has been an international organization that promotes food culture as an alternative to fast food. It has these aims: encourage farming, preserve food traditions, and protect cultivation techniques. It was established as part of the Slow Movement. However, it has since grown as a movement in its own right. There are offices in eight countries: Italy, Germany, Switzerland, the U.S.A., France, Japan, Chile, and the U.K. Carlo Petrini, its founder, is still active in the movement. To spread the message to a younger generation, volunteers teach gardening skills to students.

Grammar

1

1 easier
2 more famous
3 bigger
4 better
5 wider
6 more noisily
7 more easily
8 worse
9 better
10 slower
11 faster
12 further / farther

2

2 Joe ran the race more quickly than Tom.
3 Oscar travels farther / further to school than Noor.
4 Beth's grade on the exam was worse than Alex's.
5 Chicago is hotter than New York.
6 Tim can run longer than Kenzo.
7 Chemistry 103 is more difficult than Chemistry 101.
8 An airplane ticket is more expensive than a bus ride.

WRITING TASK

I shop in both supermarkets and convenience stores. Both have their plusses and minuses, but overall I prefer to shop in convenience stores. Supermarkets are bigger than convenience stores. Therefore, they take longer to get through. I feel they are also more impersonal. There is a lot a choice in a supermarket, but I don't need all that choice. The food is fresher in supermarkets than in convenience stores. However, the lines are always longer. I can get though the lines more quickly in a convenience store. Convenience stores often stay open later, so are, of course, more convenient. The prices in convenience stores are almost always higher than in supermarkets, but I usually try to buy things on sale. In fact, there are three things I never buy in convenience stores: fruit, vegetables, and meat. If I want them, the supermarket is better.

STUDY SKILLS Keeping a journal

Scenario

Possible answer:

Fatima writes every day and she writes in a place where she feels comfortable. However, she should write more quickly and not worry so much about her grammar, spelling, and punctuation.

UNIT 7 Vision

Discussion point

Possible answers:

3 *"to tell a white lie"*
To tell a small, unimportant lie
"to see things in black and white"
To see things as all good or all bad
"to see red"
To be extremely angry
"to do something once in a blue moon"
To be something rarely
"to be in a gray area"
To be in an area that is not clearly defined
"to give someone the green light"
To give permission to do something

Vocabulary preview

1 b	3 a	5 a	7 b
2 a	4 a	6 b	8 b

READING 1 Is seeing really believing?

Global reading

1

2 Optical illusions

2

Students should have circled the following color words; red, blue, yellow, green, brown, orange.

Close reading

1 Color is created by our brains.
2 Light plays a role on how our brain perceives images.
3 In the first illusion, the colors are the same.
4 Color is created according to our past experiences.
5 We all see the world in different ways.

READING 2 Colors and flags

Before you read

White is used the most.

Global reading

1 Russia		4 Colombia
2 The United Nations		5 Mali
3 France		6 Kuwait

Close reading

2

	Meaning 1	Meaning 2
Black	strength	determination
White	peace	purity
Blue	freedom	prosperity
Red	blood	courage
Green	earth	agriculture
Yellow	sun	wealth
Red, white, and blue	freedom	revolution
Green, gold, and red	African unity	African identity
Black, white, green, and red	Arab unity	different Arab dynasties

3

1 symbolize the unity of a nation
2 "the opposite of red"
3 at least one of them appeared on the flag of every country of the world at the time
4 the race is finished
5 orange

Vocabulary skill

1

1 arrangement	4 information
2 appearance	5 depression
3 dependence	6 restriction

2

1 compose	4 conclude
2 manage	5 indicate
3 prefer	6 allow

3

1 assistance	5 enjoyment
2 replacement	6 difference
3 composition	7 confusion
4 suggestion	8 appointment

WRITING Describing colors

Writing skill

1

1 F	3 S	5 S	7 F
2 S	4 F	6 S	8 F

2

Possible answer:

The background on the South Korean flag is white because white is a traditional color of the Korean people. The blue and red circle in the center represents the origins of everything in the universe. The circle represents opposites, such as positive and negative, and night and day. The black lines around the circle represent the elements of fire, water, earth, wood, and metal. After you understand the symbolism behind this or any flag, you appreciate it more.

Grammar

1

1 gasoline, water
2 cheese, gold
3 rice, salt
4 clothing, money
5 friendship, information
6 Arabic, engineering
7 heat, weather

2

1 If you want me to make **cookies** [C], please buy some **flour** [N] and **sugar** [N].
2 The **weather** [N] was terrible on our **vacation** [C]. There was **rain** [N] every **day** [C].
3 Our **teacher** [C] said our **homework** [N] is not due until **Tuesday** [C].
4 At my **university** [C] lots of **students** [C] study **economics** [N].
5 Can you buy some **bread** [N], **cheese** [N], **fruit** [N], and **carrots** [C].
6 This brown **furniture** [N] is not **wood** [N]. It is some kind of cheap **plastic** [N].

3

1 It takes a lot of ⟨patience⟩ to teach ⟨children⟩.
2 Iris never tells ⟨lies⟩. She always tells the ⟨truths⟩.
3 I need some ⟨advice⟩ on finding a ⟨job⟩ where I can use my ⟨English⟩.
4 The ⟨information⟩ in these ⟨brochures⟩ is not accurate.
5 That ⟨department store⟩ sells both ⟨food⟩ and ⟨furnitures⟩.
6 This ⟨meat⟩ needs ⟨salts⟩ and this ⟨sauce⟩ needs ⟨pepper⟩.
7 The ⟨color red⟩ can represent ⟨bloods⟩ and ⟨courage⟩.
8 The ⟨chemicals⟩ in the ⟨waters⟩ make it look orange.

WRITING TASK

Like many ⟨colors⟩, ⟨yellow⟩, ⟨blue⟩ and ⟨green⟩ can have different <u>meanings</u> in different <u>cultures</u>. In my <u>culture</u>, ⟨yellow⟩ often means a <u>lack</u> of ⟨bravery⟩. If you are afraid of something, you might be considered "<u>yellow</u>." We also have an <u>expression</u> "yellow ⟨journalism⟩." This refers to ⟨journalism⟩ that is not always 100% true. ⟨Yellow⟩ is also used to mean slow down since it's the middle <u>color</u> on traffic <u>lights</u>. The color ⟨blue⟩ can represent ⟨sadness⟩. For <u>example</u>, the <u>expressions</u> "to feel blue" and "to have the <u>blues</u>" mean to feel very sad. The <u>color</u> ⟨green⟩ can have several <u>meanings</u> in my <u>culture</u>. It can symbolize ⟨spring⟩, ⟨growth⟩ and ⟨nature⟩. It can represent ⟨recycling⟩ and ⟨environmentalism⟩. It can even represent ⟨money⟩ because our ⟨currency⟩ is green. Also, if you say someone is "green" it means that they don't have very much ⟨experience⟩. I'm not sure why we say that!

UNIT 8 Extremes

Discussion point

1 b 2 b 3 a

Vocabulary preview

1 firsthand	6 operate
2 convince	7 dedicated
3 species	8 investigate
4 eventually	9 expedition
5 concerned	

READING 1 Earth's final frontier

Global reading

1 11		3 2010		5 11,033
2 26.7		4 7,000		

Close reading

1

Highlighted words that indicate similarities:
like, also, neither, both
Highlighted words that indicate differences:
while, however, whereas, but

2

Alvin
named after a researcher
can dive for nine hours
is 7 meters long

Both
investigates new species
maps the ocean floor
operates in global waters
researches underwater earthquakes

Shinkai
can dive to 6,500 meters
holds two pilots and a researcher
is 9.5 meters long

READING 2 Super Sherpa

Before you read

Possible answer:

The picture shows trash on a mountain. It was taken on Mount Everest. It was left there by people who had climbed the mountain.

Global reading

3 Environmental newsmagazine

Close reading

1

1 M 2 S 3 M 4 S 5 M 6 S 7 M

2

1 They're known for their ability to carry heavy loads for long distances at high altitudes.
2 He climbed Mount Everest for the first time in 1990.
3 It said, "Stop Climate Change."
4 He founded the Apa Sherpa Foundation, which is dedicated to improving the education and economic development of the Nepalese people.
5 He is known as the "Super Sherpa" for the ease with which he climbs mountains.

3

Statements that you can infer: 2, 3, 5

Vocabulary skill

1

1	mother ship	6	primary school
2	shipwreck	7	uphill
3	earthquake	8	mountain climber
4	ocean floor	9	firsthand
5	hometown	10	climate change

2

1	baseball	4	breakfast
2	stop sign	5	overtime
3	workout		

3

Possible answers:

1 airplane, airport, airline, airfare, aircraft, air pressure, air force
2 bookcase, bookend, bookshelf, bookmark, bookstore book bag, book review
3 understand, underwater, underground, underneath, underline, undercover
4 headache, headline, headquarters, headphones, headway, headband, head start

WRITING Giving your opinion

Writing skill

1

1 There are many in the Caribbean Sea as well.
2 Moreover, a sea is surrounded by land.
3 In addition, it is the largest by volume.
4 It is also one of the most shallow.
5 The blue whale is the largest and heaviest mammal.

2

1	clearly / certainly	3	clearly / certainly
2	Above all	4	In fact

Grammar

1

1	cannot	4	could
2	could not	5	can
3	am not able to	6	cannot

2

Possible answers:

1 I cannot swim.
2 Ben was not able to make it to the top of the mountain.

---

3 Kamal is able to name over a hundred types of tropical fish.
4 My brother and I were able to go camping by ourselves as kids.
5 Richard could not win his first swimming race last month.

WRITING TASK

Team sports such as baseball and volleyball <u>can teach</u> us a lot about life. First, sports <u>can show</u> us that we need to work hard. For example, we may need to pace ourselves (and) (have) endurance to achieve our aims. (In addition) practice is important if we want to be good at a sport. I <u>couldn't play</u> basketball well in high school but I kept practicing and now I <u>can play</u> well. Second, sports clearly prepare students for the real world. Players learn how to work together and get along. They learn how to solve problems (as well.) (In fact) all of these are essential skills for working in any business or organization. Third, sports (also) teach us about failing. Winning isn't everything. Every game or sport will have a winner and a loser, and sports <u>are able to teach</u> us that it's OK to lose sometimes, if you try your best. (Moreover,) we often learn more from our failures than our successes.

STUDY SKILLS Using computers for effective study

Scenario

Possible answer:

Ingrid drafts and edits her work, and she checks her spelling and grammar. However, she would save a lot of time if she used the computer because she would not have to write out her assignment again. She could also use the computer spell and grammar check functions.

UNIT 9	Life

Vocabulary preview

1	adolescent	5	capability
2	familiar	6	resistant
3	Discard	7	transition
4	technical	8	sustain

READING 1 Coming of age

Global reading

The text will be about the adolescent and teen years.

Close reading

1	adult	5	driver's license
2	passage	6	ceremony
3	preparation	7	diving
4	recognized	8	responsibility

READING 2 Gardening 380 kilometers above Earth

Global reading

3 Growing plants in space

Close reading

1

Possible answer:

Astronauts are growing plants in space. It is expensive to send anything to space so this

---

saves money. Plants are a renewable food source, and they improve air quality. There are some challenges with growing plants in space, especially the lack of gravity and the need for soil. However, the use of fans and special gels are helping overcome the challenges. Scientists are also working on the plants. They are breeding them to grow more efficiently and be disease resistant. These innovations may also improve life on Earth.

2

1 They wanted familiar foods to ease their transition to foreign lands.
2 The trips can be very long, and it is expensive to send anything into space.
3 They use carbon dioxide and produce oxygen.
4 It stays around the plants because of the lack of gravity.
5 They use gels because soil is too heavy to send to space.

3

1

a early explorers b early explorers

2

a the oxygen
b the plants

3

a special gels b water

Vocabulary skill

1

a 2 b 3 c 1

2

a 2 b 3 c 5 d 1 e 4

WRITING Describing a memorable day

Writing skill

1

1 after; Meanwhile; later
2 When; Before; at the same time
3 First; Second; Before
4 once; While; as soon as

2

Possible answers:

1 watch TV
2 chat with my friends
3 get text messages
4 take another one
5 sitting at her desk
6 close my book and go home

Grammar

1

1 got; had
2 did not go; broke
3 bought; shared
4 retired; worked
5 told; did not lose; turned

2

1	felt	5	did not find
2	took	6	studied
3	stood	7	held
4	got	8	screamed

WRITING TASK

I remember my high school graduation very well. Besides my immediate family, a lot of my aunts, uncles, and cousins <u>came</u> to the ceremony. I <u>put</u> on my graduation gown and cap and we all <u>drove</u> to the ceremony. It <u>didn't</u> <u>last</u> very long. Some people <u>gave</u> speeches and (then) they <u>presented</u> awards. We all just <u>sat</u> there quietly (during) all that. (Next) they <u>handed</u> us our diplomas. (While) we <u>stood</u> in line to receive them, my mother <u>took</u> a lot of photos and my brother <u>tried</u> to make me laugh. I think my mom <u>cried</u> a little. (Once) I got my diploma, I <u>felt</u> really fantastic. (After) everyone <u>had</u> their diplomas, we all <u>threw</u> our graduation caps up in the air. That's a fun tradition. (Later) at home, my friends and family <u>gave</u> me cards and presents. I <u>had</u> a great day.

STUDY SKILLS Making the most of your dictionary

Scenario

Possible answer:

Kwame uses the guidewords to find words quickly and looks for the correct definition. However, he does not study the pronunciation.

UNIT 10 Work

Vocabulary preview

1 to reverse
2 close
3 appearance
4 annoyed
5 downgrade
6 detailed
7 average
8 easy

READING 1 The farmer's lazy son

Global reading

1

1 Someone will find a way to get Paolo to work.

Close reading

1

a 2 b 4 c 6 d 7 e 9 f 12
g 1 h 8 i 11 j 3 k 10 l 5

2

inform, entertain

READING 2 Leave it for the robot

Before you read

Picture 1: preparing food / cooking
Picture 2: factory work
Picture 3: exploring

Global reading

1

The text is about different types of robots, and what they can do for us.

2

1 millions
2 mechanical arm
3 explore the surface of the moon and Mars; perform maintenance on oil drilling platforms (also: explore the ocean floors, gather information on geographical changes in volcanoes)
4 vacuums

Close reading

1

1 Spain   2 Japan   3 Germany

2

1 window cleaning   3 sports partner
2 around 60%

Vocabulary skill

1

1 b 2 d 3 c 4 a 5 h 6 g 7 e 8 f

2

1 the housework   6 work
2 a decision   7 sorry
3 a promise   8 an apology
4 thanks   9 a break
5 married   10 a favor

3

1 lunch   6 a visit
2 ready   7 a taxi
3 the laundry   8 calm
4 a mistake   9 the answer
5 overseas   10 energy

WRITING Describing your future

Writing skill

1

1 In 1939, a robot named *Elektro* was able to <u>walk</u>, <u>count</u> on its fingers, and <u>spoke</u> words.
2 Most robots today are used to doing jobs that are <u>repetitive</u>, <u>mundane</u>, or <u>danger</u>.
3 Robots are also used in factories to build things like <u>cars</u>, <u>appliances</u>, and <u>make electronics.</u>
4 Some robots are designed to <u>explore</u> underwater, <u>go</u> down into volcanoes, and <u>traveling</u> to other planets.
5 Robots have been sent to Mars to <u>collect</u> soil, rock and atmosphere samples, <u>analyze</u> them, and then <u>will send</u> the data back to Earth.
6 Another reason we use robots is because they never <u>get</u> sick, <u>take</u> a day off, or <u>complained</u>!
7 Most robots usually have at least three main parts—the "brain" <u>that is run by a computer program</u>, mechanical parts <u>that make the robot move</u>, and sensors <u>to tell the robot about its surroundings</u>.
8 Unlike in TV programs, robots are unable to <u>think</u>, <u>feel</u>, or <u>makes</u> decisions.

2

1 In 1939, a robot named *Elektro* was able to walk, count on its fingers, and speak words.
2 Most robots today are used to doing jobs that are repetitive, mundane, or dangerous.
3 Robots are also used in factories to build things like cars, appliances, and electronics.
4 Some robots are designed to explore underwater, go down into volcanoes, and travel to other planets.
5 Robots have been sent to Mars to collect soil, rock and atmosphere samples, analyze them, and then send the data back to Earth.
6 Another reason we use robots is because they never get sick, take a day off, or complain!
7 Most robots usually have at least three main parts – the "brain" that is run by a computer program, mechanical parts that make the robot move, and sensors that tell the robot about its surroundings.
8 Unlike in TV programs, robots are unable to think, feel, or make decisions.

Grammar

1

1 d 2 a 3 c 4 b

2

1 will finish   4 will quit
2 will work   5 will look
3 will not / won't rain   6 will do

3

Possible answers:

Robots will replace teachers.
People will only work 20 hours a week.
People will not use money.
There will be a cure for cancer.

WRITING TASK

I think that my future <u>will be</u> very bright. I'm currently in my third year of college and next year I <u>will be</u> a senior. After I graduate, I <u>will</u> probably <u>travel</u> for a couple of weeks, see some friends, and then ~~to~~ look for a job. I'm studying to be an engineer so I would like to get a job in an engineering firm in my hometown. It <u>won't be</u> easy, but I <u>will do</u> my best. In three years I think I <u>will try</u> to buy a house. I want a house that is near my parents, that isn't too expensive, and that isn't far from work. I don't know, but I hope I <u>will be</u> married in four years. I'd like to start a family in about five years. I'm sure I <u>will have</u> a lot of children someday. That's what I think <u>will happen</u>, but of course no one can predict the future!